THE ENCYCLOPEDIA OF PET RABBITS

DAVID ROBINSON

ISBN 0-87666-911-9

Distributed in the U.S. by T.F.H. Publications, Inc., 211 West Sylvania
Avenue, PO Box 427, Neptune, NJ 07753; in England by T.F.H. (Gt. Britain)
Ltd., 13 Nutley Lane, Reigate, Surrey; in Canada to the book store and
library trade by Beaverbooks Ltd., 150 Lesmill Road, Don Mills, Ontario M38
2T5, Canada; in Canada to the pet trade by Rolf C. Hagen Ltd., 3225 Sartelon
Street, Montreal 382, Quebec; in Southeast Asia by Y.W. Ong, 9 Loring 36
Geylang, Singapore 14; in Australia and the South Pacific by Pet Imports
Pty. Ltd., P.O. Box 149, Brookvale 2100, N.S.W. Australia. Published by
T.F.H. Publications, Inc., Ltd., The British Crown Colony of Hong Kong.

Contents

Cover photo by Ray Hanson.

Frontis: A rabbit with Dutch pattern. Photo by L. van der Meid.

Color photos:
Dr. Herbert R. Axelrod: 48, 249
William O. Cawley (Poultry Specialist, Texas A & M University System): 281.
Armin Bierden: 41, 44, 156, 172, 173, 177
Ray Hanson: 37, 52, 61, 64, 68, 72, 76, 77, 84, 92, 93, 96, 97, 105, 112, 132, 136, 148, 149, 152, 153, 156, 160, 161, 165, 168, 173, 176, 180, 192, 193, 216, 225, 228, 229, 244, 260, 264, 265, 268, 272
Max Shaddix (Photographer, Texas Agricultural Extension Service, Texas A & M University): 52, 53, 56, 57, 65, 69, 72, 73, 80, 81, 85, 100, 101, 108, 109, 112, 113, 116, 117, 120, 121, 124, 125, 128, 129, 136, 137, 144, 145, 148, 169, 172, 181, 184, 185, 188, 189, 193, 200, 204, 205, 208, 209, 212, 217, 220, 224, 228, 232, 233, 236, 237, 240, 241, 244, 245, 248, 257, 272, 281
Claudia Watkins: 141
World of Pets: 33, 36, 68, 80, 89, 124, 128, 133, 181, 184, 201, 224, 252, 256, 288
Author: 56, 57, 76, 81, 84, 88, 89, 101, 120, 121, 137, 157, 164, 165, 169, 189, 196, 197, 201, 213, 216, 221, 233, 240, 245, 249, 253, 273, 276, 277, 280, 288

Black and White photos:
Albers Milling Co., 43; Dr. Herbert R. Axelrod, 70; Louise Boyle, 7; Cooper Breesport, 282; Kraig Carpenter, 226; Paul Ingram, 278; Everett E. Lund, 304; George Pickow (Three Lions, Inc.); 14, 17, 94, 255, 295, 296, 297, 299, 300, 313; Mervin F. Roberts, 66, 67; Bonnie Sanders, 246; Audrey Smith, 234; W.J. Suffried, 182; STEMO, 118; Thomas, 242; Louise van der Meid, 2; Author, 10, 28, 29, 30, 35, 50, 51, 95, 99, 103, 110, 114, 126, 127, 156, 230, 231, 255, 262, 263, 291, 310, 317

Introduction

Rabbits make good pets. They are clean, docile and intelligent. Rabbits can be kept as pets where it is impractical to keep other animals such as dogs and cats. A rabbit can be housed in the simplest of pens, it makes little or no noise and, if properly looked after, it does not smell. Only the basics are needed to maintain a rabbit in good condition: a warm, dry pen or hutch; clean, wholesome food; and fresh water to drink.

It is unfortunate that many pet rabbits are maltreated by their well-meaning owners because of the owners' ignorance or complacency. Rabbits are often bought as pets for young children. Once the child loses interest in the pet, the poor animal is neglected, and the responsibility for caring for it often falls on the parents. The young rabbit grows so fast that it can treble its size and weight in a few weeks. It is necessary to emphasize this harsh reality to the prospective pet rabbit owner.

The decision to buy a child a pet rabbit should not be taken lightly. It should be given much thought and consideration. The first point to consider is what kind of rabbit would be suitable as a child's pet. Fortunately, most breeds of rabbit are medium-sized and can be handled by children without much difficulty. However, some grow to comparatively huge size and can be handled only by experienced people. It can be a great frustration to own a cuddly little baby rabbit that matures into a 10-pound adult.

The prospective pet rabbit owner should read the chapter on rabbit breeds in this book to determine the adult size and weight of various rabbits before making a purchasing decision. Visit a good local pet store and talk to the proprietor about suitable-size rabbits. Also, take a good look at the hutches and notice how well-made they are. You can also observe how clean and healthy the stock is.

If you cannot find a pet store that has rabbits labeled according to breed, the only guide is the markings that the rabbit bears. In some cases, it is very obvious that the rabbit resembles the Dutch or English breeds. When the markings are entirely black or blue, with just a smudge of white here and there, you may try weighing the rabbit and comparing the weight to its approximate age.

In addition to the importance from the standpoint of ease of handling, the size of the rabbit is an important consideration in the size and type of hutch to be provided. It would be futile to buy a pen or hutch that will provide enough room only while the rabbit is a baby. In a few weeks the growing rabbit would outgrow its home. The ideal-size pen should measure at least four feet by three feet, the larger the better, of course.

Hutches and pens can be purchased at or ordered from most good pet stores. If you cannot find a pen at your local pet store, it is possible to construct one, but it must be carefully made in order to protect the rabbit from bad weather and also make cleaning a simple job.

Many pet rabbits are housed in dilapidated hutches. The rabbit can easily escape from these, and the poor animal also suffers when the weather turns bad. Cleaning becomes a detested chore that it is often postponed until the rabbit falls ill from diseases bred in the damp and caked hutch litter.

Ideally, there should be no part of the hutch that the rabbit can chew. All projections should be protected by tacking strips of metal along the leading edges.

Some of the best materials for hutch-making include exterior-quality plywood, timber and brick. Materials that are not recommended are hardboard, chipboard and flakeboard. These materials are not intended for outside use and will quickly deteriorate under outdoor conditions. Even if they are well protected on the outside, the buildup of the rabbit's urine on the inside will have a rotting effect.

If the potential rabbit owner lives in a warm, dry climate, the best material available is wire. Wire can be cut easily with special cutters, and the edges can be joined with clips applied with a pair of pliers made specifically for the job. Because the floor of the pen is also made of wire, there is no bedding to clear away. In the wire hutch, the rabbit's droppings fall through the holes and collect in

This rabbit hutch is well constructed and adequate for keeping a few small rabbits out of doors. However, the rabbit's keeper has no protection during bad weather.

a tray placed underneath the pen. This type of pen is also very popular with commercial rabbit raisers.

Whether the hutch is made of wood or wire or another material, it must have a roof that slopes from front to back. The roof must also overhang the walls of the hutch by at least three inches all around. If this point is neglected, rain can be driven into the hutch; water will run down the back wall, making conditions very damp inside. A roof tarpaulin is also essential if the roof is not to suffer from the weather. If the hutch is a solid material, it must have a wire front that covers at least half of the entire hutch front. Both halves of the front should be hinged or completely removable for ease of cleaning.

The hutch should stand where it will face the morning sun and also be sheltered from prevailing winds. The floor of the hutch should never touch the ground, as it would speed the rotting of the hutch and inhibit the flow of air underneath it. Brick or concrete block pillars can be built to keep the hutch off the ground. If a homemade hutch is built on wooden legs, the legs must be protected with preservative.

Rabbits are easy to look after if a regular routine is followed. There are no precise rules about the time of day the rabbit should be fed. Feeding is flexible, depending on how much free time the owner has. It is customary to feed a small handful of hay in the morning and the main meal of pellets or grain in the evening.

Each rabbit is different in its feeding habits. Some will clear away their food in a matter of minutes. Others will nibble at the food and even have some left over at the next feeding time. Common sense and experience will dictate how much to feed at one time. Rabbits may waste their food if they are given too much. It is best to feed a young rabbit as much as it will eat in half an hour and remove the surplus so that the rabbit will not have a chance to be wasteful. Hay can be left in the hutch at all times. It is not too filling and gives the animal something to munch on.

Clean, fresh water *must* be available at all times. It must never be allowed to stagnate. Because rabbits seem to delight in upsetting their feeding and watering pots, the water should be provided in a gravity bottle. These bottles have the advantages of being easy to fill and keeping the water clean.

Rabbit food can be purchased from pet stores in ready-mixed quantities. It is normally a mixture of pellets, oats, wheat and other small seeds. If it is good quality, it will be free from dust and dirt and will not smell musty. The rabbit food should be stored away from the hutch. Any food that falls on the ground in the vicinity of the hutch should be swept up immediately, as it would attract mice and rats.

All rabbits are naturally curious, which helps in making friends with a new pet. Upon its arrival, a pet rabbit should be introduced to its new home quietly and and without too much fuss.

The Rabbit's Place
in the World

For a long time, rabbits were taxonomically classed within the order Rodentia, a large (about 40% of the total) body of mammals that are commonly called rodents. The order Rodentia includes not only the common mouse and rat but also gerbils, hamsters, lemmings, porcupines and beavers, to name only a few others. Today zoologists consider rabbits, hares and some closely related animals to form an order of their own, the order Lagomorpha. Blood tests show that there is a lesser relationship between rodents and rabbits than previously had been thought to exist. Rodents are characterized by having teeth that grow throughout life. The teeth of rabbits, unlike man's and like rodents', are permanent and do not grow continuously. Another distinction is the presence of a bone called the bacullum in the sheath of the penis in males; it is present in rodents but not in lagomorphs.

The order Lagomorpha contains two families, the family Ochotonidae and the family Leporidae. Ochotonidae contains one genus and 13 species; Leporidae contains 9 genera and approximately 50 species. Members of the family Ochotonidae are small burrowing animals that don't look too much like rabbits. They are commonly known as pikas. They are furry, with short ears and no tail, and are found mostly in Asia, though two species are found in North America. They are also known as whistling hares because of the sharp bark or whistle that they make. The differences between rabbits and hares are slight, and there is much confusion by way of common names, the one being the name for the other, and vice versa. The only generally recognizable difference is that hares are larger than rabbits, but this is very basic.

The Belgian hare is a racy type of rabbit breed and should not be allowed to get fat through lack of exercise and giving the wrong kind of food.

Members of the family Leporidae (both rabbits and hares) have a sensory pad situated at the entrance of each nostril. They are basically helpless against some predators and depend on their senses of smell and hearing to protect them by providing warning. The hind limbs are longer than the fore limbs; rabbits and hares drum with their feet as a means of communication.

The rabbit is much admired all over the world for many reasons. It is tenacious and can survive against almost all odds, whether predators, disease or famine. Because of its high fertility rate, the rabbit has been able to maintain its population at a constant level except through man's intervention.

Rabbits can be found in many places over the earth, from the desert regions of the East and West to frozen polar wastes. The Romans were the first to realize the value of the rabbit as a commodity. The rabbit was easy to transport in crates, so it became a staple food of the great Roman armies as they swept across Europe.

The fact that the rabbit is so widespread is a tribute to its tenacity and adaptability. Many rabbits must have escaped from the flimsy wooden crates that served as their quarters. It is also possible that some rabbits were deliberately set free to provide sport and entertainment for the bored troops. It would only be a matter of time before these fugitives began to breed and multiply.

A classic example of the rabbit's adaptability and rapid breeding occurred on the island of Porto Santo in the Madeira Islands chain in 1418. The Portugese set rabbits free on the island, and the rabbits multiplied in such numbers that the island had to be abandoned by the human community. A modern example occurred in Australia, where rabbits were introduced from England. The rabbit soon became a serious pest, and the virus disease myxomatosis was deliberately introduced to curb the rabbit population.

The Romans used stone walls to confine their rabbit herds. Although the method seems crude compared to contemporary hutches and pens, the Romans were able to control their herds and keep their numbers at the desired level.

Selective breeding of rabbits did not begin until about one thousand years after Roman power had begun to decline. The first written accounts of selective breeding were recorded by French monks in about the 14th century. Selective breeding had two important effects: bigger meat rabbits could be produced and new colors could be bred in the form of mutants. This was the birth of the rabbit fancy as we know it today.

The rabbit is also an important figure in fables, folklore and superstition. The Romans believed that rabbit meat was an important beauty aid for their women. The Chinese sacrificed rabbits to the gods with the hope that their crops of rice and fruit would be as bountiful as rabbits' offspring. Our own Easter bunny is, according to some, derived from an ancient fable in which a rabbit laid a clutch of colored eggs for a spring festival.

Rabbits also played an important role in witchcraft. They were thought to have the ability to ward off evil spirits. In the Middle Ages, belief in witchcraft was quite common. There was a superstition in England that the victim of the devil and evil spirits need only hang the left hind foot of a rabbit around his neck at midnight on the night of the full moon to protect himself. Different parts of the rabbit had other uses in warding off evil.

The development of the rabbit from its natural form and environment has been almost exclusively due to the influence of man. Man has developed and bred rabbits to serve his own needs as meat and fur producers and as a pet and exhibition animal.

The fancy rabbit has been exhibited at shows since the early nineteenth century. From France, where the fancy rabbit originated, it spread to England and Scandinavia. The most popular fancy rabbit of this period was undoubtedly the Belgian hare. The popularity of this breed resulted from two characteristics: it was a fancy rabbit and it was large and therefore useful for meat production.

It was the Belgian hare that began to attract people to the rabbit in the United States. The Belgian hare was introduced around 1900, and shortly after that came the Belgian hare boom.

Gradually other fancy breeds became popular, and so did the fur breeds. In addition to being an exhibition animal, the rabbit was developed somewhat as a meat and fur producer and, of course, as a pet.

As fur became increasingly fashionable, it was discovered that precious furs such as chinchilla and silver fox could be imitated with rabbit skins.

The popularity of the rabbit as a meat producer has remained rather limited. The commercial rabbit industry in England has never been big. Perhaps this was due to the spread of the deadly rabbit disease myxomatosis that ravaged the English rabbit and made the idea of rabbit meat repulsive to many housewives. In the United States, rabbit meat has met with more success, particularly as a home-grown food.

Anatomy and Physiology

The rabbit has been used in research for many years. Students have learned a great deal about the human body through studies of the rabbit's anatomy. Many of the rabbit's internal organs work on the same principle as human organs. For this reason, the rabbit is used as a biology subject for school children all over the world. Rabbit physiology has also been an aid in the scientific search for new and better ways of treating and curing human diseases.

EXTERNAL FEATURES

The rabbit is about the same size as the body of an adult domestic cat—between 15 and 18 inches long from the tip of the nose to the tip of the tail. The head is round, but the face is slightly elongated. The nostrils, or nares, are small and encircled with a small, bare, moist area of skin called rhinarium.

The relatively large mouth is bordered by lips that can be separated to show the top pair of incisor teeth. The top part of the lip is cleft at the front. The area around the mouth and cheeks of the rabbit is covered with long fine whiskers or vibrissae. There are also vibrissae around the eyes.

The rabbit's eyes are large and set laterally. The very prominent pupils give a field of vision of 360 degrees. It is interesting to note that the eyes have fields of vision that overlap at the front by about 30 degrees and at the back by about 10 degrees.

The rabbit has three eyelids: an upper eyelid, a lower eyelid and a third eyelid that can be closed to protect the cornea during fighting or dust storms. Both the upper and lower eyelids have eyelashes. The top pair is unusually long.

The most prominent feature of the rabbit's head is the elongated ears or pinnae. Under normal conditions the ears remain erect.

13

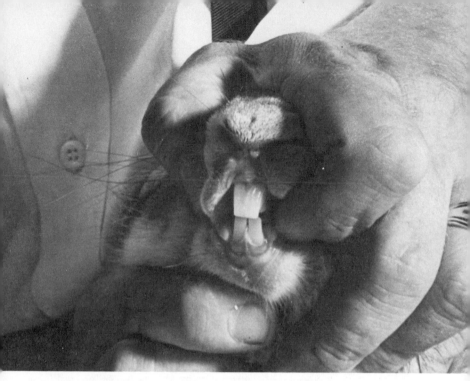

An adult rabbit held in a manner that the lower and upper pairs of cutting teeth or incisors are visible. When teeth are misaligned uneven growth of the teeth or malocclusion results.

When the rabbit is running, fighting or frightened, the ears are lowered and laid back along the lines of the body out of harm's way.

The head is separated from the body by a short neck which is barely visible when distended. A rabbit's forelimbs are thin and fine in structure. When the rabbit is in a crouched position, they are held slightly bent at the joint of the elbow just underneath the chest.

The chest or thorax is separated from the abdomen by a midriff or diaphragm. Inside the chest cavity, well protected by a bony rib cage, are the heart and lungs of the rabbit.

The lower abdomen has a permanently constricted wall of muscle to protect the organs contained inside. The flexible spine or backbone consists of seven cervical (neck) vertebrae, twelve thoracic (chest) vertebrae and seven lumbar (trunk) vertebrae. Three sacral vertebrae and many tiny caudals give support to the tail. The spine is joined to the rest of the rabbit skeleton at the shoulder girdle and the pelvic girdle.

The rabbit's hind limbs are elongated and very strong. They play an important role in the everyday life of the wild rabbit. Most important is their use in running. They provide the rabbit with a great burst of speed. The hind limbs are also used to excavate the earth when the rabbit is digging its underground burrow. They are not actually used in the digging process, but function as shovels to remove the surplus soil that the digging rabbit piles underneath its body. The soil is flung backward with the hind legs, keeping the burrow entrance clear.

Fighting plays an important role in the way of life of the male rabbit or buck. His hind feet are equipped with four long and powerful toes, each armed with strong and sharp claws. During a fight, the rabbits grapple and try to disembowel each other with slashing actions of the hind feet. The forefeet, which have five toes, are used as secondary weapons and are sometimes used to scratch the opponent's face.

The tail, which is very small, is kept tucked under the posterior. It is composed of a series of small flexible bones that form part of the spine. The tail is covered with soft, dense fur and is sometimes used as a signaling device, especially by the female rabbit.

The Fur

The rabbit has fur and skin with very specialized functions that play a vital part in the animal's physiology. They are:
1. Protection of the body against wear from external friction.
2. Reduction of the loss of body fluids by the drying process of of the air.
3. Temperature regulation.
4. The reception of external stimuli, such as heat, cold and touch.
5. Protection of the body from harmful rays of the sun.
6. Protection of the body from germs and bacteria.

The epidermis of the skin contains hair follicles from the base of which the single fiber of hair grows. The cells contained in the epidermis are always active. As they are pushed to the surface of the skin by new cell growth, they keratinize and die. Each hair is a structure of these dead cells, which contain air pockets and have scaly walls. It is the scaly walls that make the fur cling together when stroked. A fatty secretion emitted from the base of each hair by the cells in the lower layer of skin, or dermis, waterproofs the fur.

Grooming is an essential part of the rabbit's toilet. Its main function is to keep the fur in its best possible condition at all times. This is achieved by the removal of dead hairs and the coating of the whole fur with saliva from the rabbit's mouth to extract the dust and dirt.

The rabbit does not sweat through the skin of the body, but from a sweat gland situated on the underside of each forepaw.

The hairs are controlled by muscles that determine the angle at which the hair lies when contracted or expanded. It is possible for the rabbit to regulate its body temperature by controlling the amount of air trapped within the fur. The trapped air is heated by the rabbit's body to help keep the skin warm.

As each hair wears away, it is replaced by the active cells of the epidermis as new cells are created, pushing the old ones to the surface, where they die and form part of the hair structure. There are two types of hair on the rabbit: the undercoat, which is scale-covered and soft to the touch, and the guard hairs, which are harsh to the touch. The guard hairs are slightly longer than the undercoat hairs and are not scale-covered to the extreme tips but culminate in an enlarged tip.

The molt, or shedding of the coat, occurs annually. The coat is shed in a variety of ways, depending on the age of the rabbit. In the young rabbit, the coat is shed at about eight weeks and is replaced by what is called the intermediate coat. At about five to six months of age, this coat is subsequently shed and replaced by the adult coat, which is much darker in color than the previous two coats.

The adult rabbit molts only once a year, beginning in early spring and finishing in October. Some rabbits will molt so quickly that they are finished by the end of June. Many of these rabbits will molt again before the end of the year.

The female or doe undergoes another form of molt. Hormonal activity during pregnancy loosens the hairs of the belly so that the

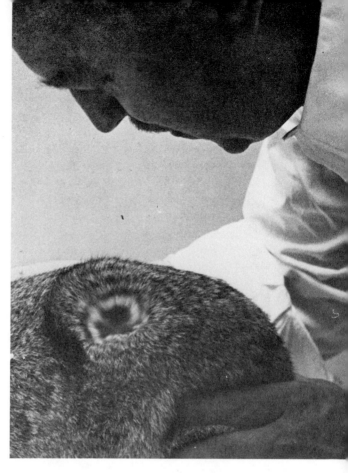

By blowing directly on the fur, the hairs are parted and the hair pattern is seen. This is the fur of a chinchilla rabbit, a popular fur breed.

doe can pluck them from her body to line the nest when the expected litter arrives. This also serves to expose the mammary glands so that the newborn litter can suckle. This happens every time the doe conceives, whether the young are stillborn or born alive.

Pet rabbits exhibit four distinct types of fur: normal, angora, rex and satin. A normally furred rabbit has slightly longer guard hairs than undercoat hairs. This fur is soft or hard, depending on whether the coat is rollback or flyback. In an angora rabbit both the guard hairs and the undercoat are elongated and wavy, giving the whole coat a woolly appearance. In rex rabbits the guard hairs are reduced to the length of the undercoat and sometimes are even shorter; the fur has a plush velvety texture. Satin fur is more lustrous and gives more intense color.

THE SKELETON

The skeleton of a typical rabbit is made up mostly of hard bone, but there are certain parts (such as the tail and limb joints) which are flexible for ease of movement.

The Skull

The rabbit skull is long and narrow. The main part of the skull is made up of the lower and upper parts of the jaw. The upper jaw contains the long nasal passages, which reach almost as far as the eyes. The bone in the upper jaw is a catacomb of air pockets and is very light in weight.

The lower jaw has strong cheekbones and a long dental ridge along which there are six cheek teeth. Both the lower and upper jaws have chisel-like teeth, two pairs at the top and one at the bottom. The top pairs are situated one behind the other. The top cheek teeth consist of five molars. There are 28 teeth in total. The tympanic bullae or inner ear cavities are also enlarged and contain the complicated nerve sensors of the ears.

The brain cavity or brain pan is comparatively small in proportion to the size of the skull. This may suggest that the rabbit relies on impulse rather than thought as a means of motivation.

The Spinal Column

The spinal column is the main supporting feature of the rabbit's skeleton. It supports the weight of the chest and abdomen and also joins the top and bottom parts of the body. The spine is also quite flexible for ease of body movement. It is made up of a number of interlocking vertebrae. The limbs are joined to the spine by the shoulder and pelvic girdles.

The shoulder girdle is a simple device made up of a triangular plate of bone with a ridge of cartilage running along the dorsal edge. Where the shoulder joins the humerus the girdle is hollow, allowing the joint to swivel. The girdle is not, in fact, joined directly onto the spine, but is embedded in muscle.

The pelvic girdle, which is in two halves, is fused to the spine itself. The girdle is joined to the femur by a joint that gives the leg limited flexibility.

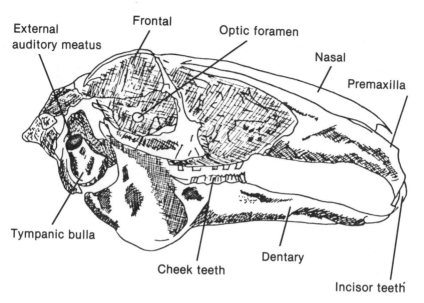

Skull of a rabbit.

Skeleton of a rabbit.

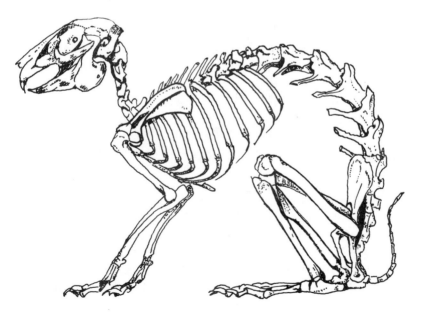

The Forelimbs

The forelimbs or front legs of the rabbit have considerable rotation because of the ball-like joints of the humerus, where they are attached to the shoulder girdle. The muscle along the humerus forms a pulley at the distal end that bends the joint where the radius and ulna of the forearm join it. The radius and ulna, although separate, cannot move independently.

The wrist of the rabbit's forearm consists of eight bones. These bones all interlock and have only limited flexibility. There are five metacarpals or fingers. The first digit has two joints; the others have three joints.

The Rib Cage

The rabbit has 24 ribs, twelve on each side of the chest cavity. The main function of the rib cage is to protect the lungs and heart of the rabbit from any undue pressure or blows. The ribs are joined to the spine by movable joints with cartilaginous pads so that they remain rigid but pliable enough to move slightly when the lungs expand during inhalation.

The Hind Limbs

The hind leg bone or femur is joined to the pelvic girdle at an angle. This enables the rabbit to bend the hind limbs comfortably when sitting in the normal crouched position. The femur is joined to the tibiofibula by way of a hinged joint which is covered with a kneecap to protect the tendons. The ankle contains six bones that are joined to four metatarsals or toes. The hind foot has an almost non-existent first toe. The other toes each have three joints.

THE MUSCLES

The muscles of the rabbit are too numerous to detail. The major ones are those that are attached to the spine and provide up and down and sideways movement. The muscles at the major joints are antagonistically arranged so that one muscle flexes the joint and another one straightens it. The muscles are made up of strands of fibers and are connected to the bone of the joint they control.

No joint in the rabbit's body is controlled by a single pair of muscles. Each joint is covered with a sheath of muscle which contains a fluid and joint cartilage.

THE BLOOD SYSTEM

Typical of all mammals, the rabbit has a complete double circulation system. The main feature of the blood system is the heart. The rabbit's heart is divided into four chambers: two auricles and two ventricles. The left and right auricles are thin-walled so that they can be moved by the low blood pressure of the veins.

The ventricles are thick-walled because they pump blood from the heart. The blood returning from the body enters the right auricle, flows into the right ventricle, and is pumped out of the heart to the lungs via the pulmonary artery. In the lungs the blood is aerated and returns to the left auricle via the pulmonary vein, flows into the left auricle, and is pumped through the aorta to be distributed to all parts of the body. This is a cycle that is repeated 200 times a minute in the rabbit and 70 times a minute in man.

The blood contains oxygen, foodstuffs and other chemicals absorbed. The cells of the body tissues absorb from the blood whatever substances they need. In return the blood collects from the tissue cells waste products which are then taken by the blood to the pertinent excretory organ; lung, kidney, etc. The cycle is completed by the blood returning to the heart, back into the lungs and once more into the heart before being pumped into the arteries.

DIGESTION

The process of digestion is the breaking down of food substances into particles that can be absorbed into the rabbit's body. The food is broken down by enzymes that are produced in the digestive system. The food is chewed and thoroughly mixed with the saliva from the mouth before being swallowed and passed down to the gullet. The stomach walls produce the enzymes, which initiate the process of breaking up the food.

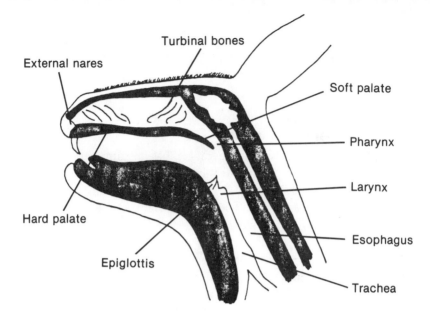

Longitudinal section of the head of a rabbit showing the respiratory passages.

When the food is pushed into the first part of the small intestine, another enzyme is mixed with it, as well as bile from the liver. The bile is a strong alkali that breaks down the fatty substance of the food into liquid form. The food is digested further as it makes its way along the entire length of the small intestine and is absorbed fully.

The absorption process entails transferring the food into the blood and distributing it to all parts of the body.

The undigested food and fiber particles pass into the caecum, where they are attacked by bacteria. Here the tough parts are digested. All the remaining matter is waste; this waste is passed to the rectum by way of the colon and excreted from the anus in the form of a fecal pellet.

Coprophagy

Coprophagy is an aspect of digestion that deserves special treatment. Coprophagy is reingestion of the soft fecal pellet that has been discharged from the anus. The feces are reingested, which is

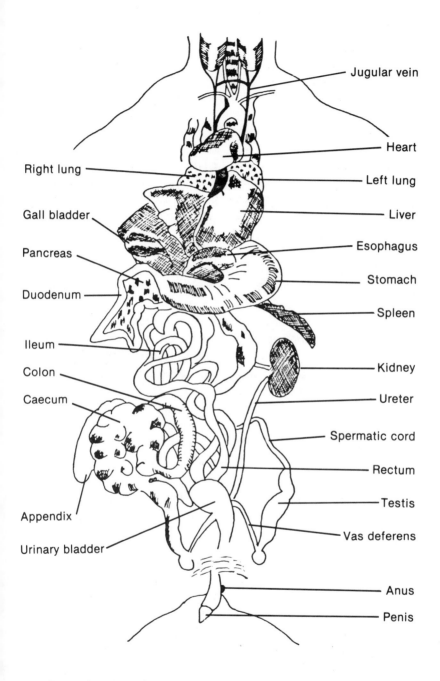

Internal organs of a rabbit.

another way of chewing the cud. Chewing the cud is a phenomenon usually associated with grazing animals such as cattle, sheep, goats, deer and even the giraffe. In all of these animals, the cud (or partly digested food) is brought up from the stomach into the mouth by muscular action. It is then chewed, and the re-chewed food travels back down the gullet to be redigested in the stomach.

The caecum or blind pouch is the largest segment of the digestive tract of a rabbit. It joins the end of the small intestine and the first segment of the colon. The digested food passes from the caecum to the colon and is excreted through the anus as soft pellets which are eaten again.

The actual eating of these soft fecal pellets is very swift and can be seen only by the observer who knows what to look for. The rabbit's hind legs part slightly and the head is pushed between them for easy access to the soft pellet.

The pellet is not always chewed. It is sometimes swallowed whole, with the entire operation completed within a matter of seconds. The pellet is contained within a membrane that encloses a fluid containing bacteria. Because the soft pellet contains a high percentage of protein, coprophagy may be a means of extracting as much protein as possible from the foodstuffs.

The fecal ingestion process may also be a way of satisfying the rabbit's hunger while it is confined underground by bad weather or the presence of predators outside the burrow.

It is also interesting that hard pellets and digested matter are not evacuated within a wild rabbit's burrow; they are instead deposited just outside the burrow, within the limits of the rabbit's territory.

RESPIRATION

The rabbit's lungs are situated in the thoracic cavity. Air is drawn into them through the trachea or windpipe. The lungs are composed of a spongy substance; each lung carries a pulmonary artery and a pulmonary vein. The trachea splits into two bronchial tubes. Each tube enters the lungs, where it in turn splits into many branches. These branches also branch out and end in tiny air sacs. Gaseous exchanges occur within the air sacs as air is drawn into them and carbon dioxide is expelled.

The action of the lungs occurs as follows: The air is drawn into the air passages of the mouth and nasal cavities and down into the lungs. The thoracic cavity increases in length and width as the air is drawn in. This is made possible by the contraction of the radial muscles of the diaphragm. At the same time, the chest cavity increases, and the air is drawn down and into the lung branches. The gaseous exchanges take place and the radial muscles of the chest relaxes, making exhalation possible. The elastic properties of the lung tissue cause the expulsion of the used air full of carbon dioxide from the sacs. The diaphragm is pushed up when the radial muscles contract and the air is expelled through the mouth and nasal passages into the atmosphere.

THE REPRODUCTIVE SYSTEM

The reproductive system of the male rabbit consists mainly of two testes contained in scrotal sacs connected to the penis by the vas deferens or Wolffian duct. This duct is thin and muscular and carries the male sperm from the testes to the penis during the act of mating. The sperm is formed within coiled tubes enclosed within the testes.

During cold weather and the nonbreeding season, the testes of the male rabbit can be withdrawn into the abdomen by muscular contraction. The scrotal sacs that contain the male testes are visible when the testes are lowered by the rabbit.

During mating, the penis is filled with blood, erected, and projects from the sheath. The spermatozoa are pushed from the vas deferens by excited muscular contractions and expelled from the penis into the vagina of the female.

The reproductive system of the female rabbit consists mainly of two ovaries connected by the Fallopian tube to the uterus and vagina. The female produces eggs in the ovaries. The eggs periodically pass along the Fallopian tubes into the uterus. If they are not fertilized by the sperm from the male, they are shed from the vagina.

The male germ cells or spermatozoa, which are tadpole-like in appearance, swim up the Fallopian tube to meet the eggs at the upper part of the tube where fertilization takes place. The fertilized eggs, or zygotes, then travel down the Fallopian tube until they come to rest in the uterus. The fertilized egg embeds itself in the wall of the womb, where it develops into a growing embryo.

Ten hours after mating, hormones released by the female rabbit cause the unfertilized eggs to be shed. These hormones are released by the pituitary gland, which is stimulated by the excited advances of the male rabbit.

Resorption

Resorption refers to the ability of the female rabbit to absorb the growing embryos into her womb. This form of internal abortion is often overlooked when studying the rabbit.

The conflicting reports that attempt to explain this phenomenon have one thing in common: all of them point to stress. Physiological stress can result from a large number of embryos in the maiden doe or unsuitable or insufficient food. Psychological stress is perhaps more common than is realized in the domestic rabbit. It may result from bad housing, poor feeding or the strain of many litters in quick succession.

For the wild rabbit, overpopulation is a major factor in resorption of unborn litters, in addition to the stresses that affect the domestic rabbit. Myers and Poole observed that as density of numbers increased in the wild Australian rabbit, fecundity decreased. Rogers and Bramwell proved in Wales that the female rabbit has a reproduction cycle and that all litters conceived were either absorbed between 11 and 15 days of pregnancy or carried full term. Watson discovered by census in New Zealand that there is also a peak in resorption at about the 21st day and that resorption fluctuated according to the season. It has been estimated that between 50 percent and 60 percent of all litters conceived by the wild female rabbit are resorbed.

The process of resorption is still not fully understood. When the expected litter does not appear after the domestic rabbit females are mated, the breeder often believes that the doe has "missed " or that the mating was unsuccessful. It is probably just as possible that the doe did in fact conceive but resorbed the litter because of unsuitable conditions.

Hutches, Pens and Equipment

Housing rabbits correctly requires considerable thought and planning. Housing does not mean merely providing the rabbit with shelter—it is much more than that. Consideration must be given to the site and final appearance of the hutch. Nothing looks so bad as bits of wood nailed together in a slapstick fashion and called a rabbit hutch. Not only does the fancier have to look at it from the house window, but the neighbors have to endure the eyesore.

If possible, the hutches should be unobtrusive and should blend into the surroundings. This is not always feasible, so the fancier should at least ensure that his hutches look neat and are well made. They should also be maintained in good condition.

An estimated 90 percent of all domestic rabbits are housed in some type of building. Therefore, they do not present the problem of being in the open and in full view of everyone around. However, the building in which the hutches are kept should be in decent condition and present a good image. Bad housing can give the rabbit fancier and the rabbit fraternity a bad name. Bad housing is more than just unsightly; it also is expensive in the long run. A strong, well-made hutch will outlast a flimsy, badly built hutch by many years.

INDOOR HOUSING

Indoor housing is perhaps the most popular way of keeping rabbits for the serious breeder or exhibitor. The basic requirement is a well-made, draftproof, weatherproof building. Such a construction can be made from a number of different materials. Brick, stone and other mineral substances are inclined to be cold in winter but cool in summer.

Wood and wood by-products are by far the most popular choice, as they are warm in winter and also in summer. In summer, wood presents problems whenever the temperature is excessive, but this can be controlled somewhat by the use of modern insulating materials that can help to lower the interior temperature.

Purchasing a wooden building can be a very expensive prospect at the outset. Many new fanciers simply take over the family garden shed amidst protests from other members of the household. Others are a little more subtle, installing a single hutch and then gradually taking over the whole shed step by step. If a new shed is out of the question because of its cost, the fancier who is handy with a few carpentry tools can build a shed from scrap or reclaimed lumber very easily and cheaply.

The final appearance of the shed has to be taken into consideration. The building need not be an elaborate structure, but it should have a solid floor and a roof that overhangs the four walls

A good rabbit room should be well ventilated, vermin-proof and free from dampness. Doors and windows must be secure to discourage the entry of rats, mice and other animals.

A block of four hutches that are attached to the wall.

by at least three inches. The size of the building will be a matter of choice, depending on cost, the size of the breed to be kept and the number of hutches that the shed is to contain.

Because good light is a major factor in maintaining rabbits in good condition, the building should have an adequate amount of window space. If the inclusion of windows is not possible, a piece can be cut out of the roof and a skylight fitted to provide a window in the shed's ceiling. In hot weather, the skylight can be opened to provide fresh air. Another solution would be to make the roof out of sheets of corrugated plastic of the type commonly used to cover patios.

Proper ventilation is also of prime importance, but this does not mean that there should be large gaps all over. The fitting of louvered panels into the walls is undoubtedly the best way of providing fresh air. If louvers are fitted, the eaves of the shed should not be restricted, as this will prevent the flow of air from the louvers from being used to full advantage. The air from the louvers will rise as it is heated and escape through the eaves.

A series of show pens with New Zealand whites. Wire mesh walls facilitate inspection of show rabbits.

Once the shed meets the basic requirements, a few refinements can be added. An electric light is very useful during the winter months.

Preferably, the rabbit shed should face the morning sun. In this location the building will warm up quickly after a cold night. Because strong sunlight can fade the coats of colored rabbits, it would be wise to install some kind of curtain or blind. Once everything has been readied, the next problem is installing the hutches themselves. There are two ways to do this.

The first is to build the hutches as part of the building. This is done by constructing a frame along one wall and simply using the walls of the shed as part of the hutches. All that is required is that the hutches be divided and the floors built by running lengths of board the whole length of the row of intended hutches. Finally, the hutch fronts and doors can be made and put into place.

30

While this method is certainly the easiest and cheapest, there are one or two snags that are not readily apparent. First, the rabbits will chew the sides of the shed. If this practice is not kept in check, the rabbits could easily chew their way out of a thin-walled shed. This habit can be discouraged to some extent by the use of metal strips along the leading edges of the exposed timber. This is a tedious job and is not necessary if the hutches are built as a separate unit from the rest of the shed. Another disadvantage of building the hutches as part of the shed is that the rabbits are exposed to the extremes of temperature, because at least one wall of the hutch is also the exterior wall of the shed. No matter how the exterior of the shed is protected, the walls will always be damp in wet weather. These conditions will encourage colds among the stock.

The second and perhaps the better way of installing hutches is to build them separately. It is certainly much more expensive, but it is well worth the expense in the long run. Hutches built as separate units are warmer and much more easily managed. Ease of management is a great asset in any rabbitry; this is something the fancier should bear in mind when constructing hutches. Hutches built as separate units are built in a free-standing block. First the shell, which will be the basic structure, is made. The size of the hutches is determined and the number of hutches required is worked out. For example, if the hutches are to be two feet wide and two feet deep, and the shed space available measures eight feet long by six feet high, it will be evident that twelve hutches will fit nicely. The hutches can be placed along two of the inside walls, creating a corridor through the center. (A word of warning here: do not made the mistake of constructing the hutches outside the shed and then discovering that they will not fit through the entrance door. It may seem like a silly mistake, but it is one that is very often made. The whole structure can be made inside the shed if there is room.)

Many types of material are available to the do-it-yourself hutch maker. Some materials are more suitable than others. Exterior-grade plywood is perhaps the best. It is easily cut to size and can be obtained in a number of thicknesses. Interior-grade plywood is cheaper but is not so suitable. A minimum thickness of three-eighths of an inch should be sufficient, but the thicker the plywood the better, as long as the weight factor is monitored. Weight is important, because the hutches may have to be moved around in the future.

Chipboard is often condemned for use within the rabbitry because it is made of chippings of timber that are compressed and glued to form a solid material. Chipboard is very absorbent, but it is warm and not much more difficult to work than plywood, provided you have the right tools. The amount of urine passed by a rabbit can be considerable, so chipboard is vulnerable in this respect. If chipboard can be protected in some way, the difficulty can be overcome. One method of protecting chipboard would be to cover the interior of the hutch with a non-toxic preservative. Another method is to paint the interior of the hutch with creosote. But the fancier would be forced to wait until the creosote was completely dry before the stock could be housed.

Whichever material is chosen, the hutches must be well constructed if they are to withstand the wear and tear. Hutches can be nailed together very easily. For a more professional job, it is better to screw the pieces together. Metal joinery pieces can be used, but it is rather unnecessary and time-consuming.

The construction of the hutch fronts or doors also requires thought and attention if it is to be done right. The most popular design is a frame covered with wire mesh. Many kinds of wire mesh are suitable for this purpose. The cheapest and most easily obtainable is wire netting or chicken wire. There are also woven wires referred to as hardware cloth. Whatever type of wire is used, the holes must be large enough to admit plenty of light but not so large that the rabbits can poke their heads through. The wire is tacked with staples onto the inside of the hutch front or door. This is done for two reasons. First, the appearance of the hutches is enhanced if the wire edges are out of sight. Second, the wire will prevent the rabbit from chewing and damaging the hutch door.

The direction in which the door opens is also important to the smooth running of the rabbitry. There is nothing more annoying than opening a hutch door that restricts ease of movement within the shed. It can make the removal of the rabbit from the hutch very difficult, leading to accidents. The best method is to make the doors for two or three hutches into one big door that will open away from the hutch. This method has the advantage of making

Pet dealers usually keep a larger supply of rabbits, especially the white breeds, during the Easter season. However, it is not wise to give very large breeds to small children.

the interior of all two or three hutches easily accessible and will therefore speed up the feeding and cleaning. Hutch doors that drop down are also somewhat handy, but they will obstruct the entrance of the hutch directly underneath. Hutch doors that open up have the same problem regarding the hutch above. The hutch door can simply be placed in position and held with hooks or buttons. The advantage is easy access to the entire front of the hutch. The disadvantage is that with several hutch doors open at once, finding a place to set all of them can be a problem in a restricted area.

The divisions between hutches can be made from the same materials as the hutches. One method is to cut large holes in two pieces and space them two inches apart as a partition. The space between the two pieces is filled with hay or straw; thus, the partition also serves as a hay rack or manger. Wire netting partitions are another alternative. But if a doe is placed next to a buck, he will spend all of his time pacing up and down in his attempt to reach the doe on the other side. This will also cause him to urinate frequently and lose weight from incessant action.

When a small breed is kept, the hutches can be made smaller. Two single hutches can be made into a double breeding hutch by using removable partitions. The partition can be designed to run between two guides made of thin strips of wood.

Once the task of constructing and installing the hutches is complete, the layout of the shed interior can be considered. Again, this is very important if the management of the rabbits is to run smoothly and efficiently.

One consideration should be some sort of bench for inspecting rabbits. If one unit of hutches is built only half the height of the others, the top will make an ideal bench. If this is impractical, a small folding bench can be used. This type of bench folds flat against a wall and will not interfere with the day-to-day operation of the rabbitry.

Most rabbitries are constructed with the units of hutches opposite each other, forming a corridor the entire length of the building along the center. Hutches that are hidden away in odd corners of the shed are very unsatisfactory. Under no circumstances should there be any hutches along the floor of the rab-

A view along one side of a rabbitry. These hutches have doors of wire mesh stretched on a wood frame.

bitry. They would be in a permanent draft and would not be easy to get to at feeding time. If the bottom row of hutches is omitted, the space can be used as a storage place for travelling boxes and other odds and ends that find their way into even the most organized rabbitries. This space serves a double purpose, as it also allows a free flow of air to circulate along the shed floor to ventilate the hutches.

Heating the rabbitry is really a refinement, but it has practical uses as well. If the fancier wishes to breed his stock the year around, heating is desirable. The choice will depend on the amount of space to be heated and the depth of the fancier's pocket. Greenhouse heaters are most practical and cheapest to run. They use very little fuel and, once installed, give off little or no fumes.

A lop-eared dwarf rabbit. This is a medium-size breed (9-12 lbs.) and it is bred chiefly for the hobby and as an exhibition animal. A large breed (below) that is meaty and not heavy boned is preferred by commercial breeders. White rabbit fur sells better than colored types because it can be dyed into any other color desired.

The tan rabbit, like the black and tan lovingly held by this young boy, is small but a good looking breed. They have lustrous silk-like fur and tans are also available in many color varieties.

Electrical space heaters are expensive to buy and run, but they will prove most efficient. Small oil burners are by far the most popular method of heating the rabbitry. They use very little electricity and are by far the safest. Regardless of the type of heating unit used, the safety factor is very important and should never be overlooked. A fire in the rabbitry can spread very quickly. The smoke from such a fire will suffocate the rabbits long before the heat and flames can do their damage.

An artificial light is also a refinement. However, if winter breeding is to be attempted, it is a must. The correct type of cable should be used if a lead is to be taken from the house or the nearest power point. Advice can be obtained from a qualified electrical engineer. Fluorescent tubes have a much more pleasing effect than incandescent bulbs. Diffusers will give the light a softer glow and will provide the whole rabbitry with a warm feeling.

The addition of a second door to the rabbitry—often made from a wooden frame covered with wire—is very useful and may even be considered a necessity. The door permits the entry of light and fresh air. If the wire is fine enough, it will restrict flying insects and other vermin from entering the rabbitry. Cleanliness is essential in the rabbitry, and any aid to cleanliness is welcome.

The rabbitry windows can also be covered with wire instead of glass. A disadvantage is that fine-mesh wire is liable to become blocked with dust and dirt, which means that the door and windows will require constant cleaning. Rain can also be driven through the wire by strong winds.

A final word on the subject of indoor housing as regards security. There are always people who will seize the opportunity to steal valuable rabbits if they are left unguarded. Always be certain that the rabbitry is locked while you are away. A good, expensive lock will prove its value time and time again. A cheap lock is easy to undo and not worth the money. An alarm system can be installed if the rabbitry is some distance from the house. Alarms can be purchased in ready-made kits or can be made with the help of a simple wiring diagram, a few bits of wire and a house doorbell.

OUTDOOR HOUSING

Where the erection of a building is impossible, an outdoor site for rabbit hutches must be considered. Basically, the principle is the same as for indoor housing. The hutches can be made as a frame with the sides, back and front filled in. As an alternative, the block system can be used. As with the indoor housing, this is the most satisfactory method.

Whatever method is chosen, the roof must overhang the front of the hutches by at least two feet. The idea is that the fancier is sheltered from the rain in wet weather; also, the rain cannot be driven into the front of the hutches by a strong wind. The hutch roof should slope downward from front to back to make sure that the ground in front of the hutches does not become water logged. A corrugated plastic roof can again be used in order to admit plenty of light to the top row of hutches.

The problems of proper ventilation are eliminated with outdoor housing, but other problems take their place. For example, the hutches must be situated somewhere where they are sheltered from the elements. The whole structure has to be protected from the weather. There are many ways of doing this. Creosote is perhaps the cheapest and easiest substance to use. Painting with enamel can be a costly enterprise especially when the hutches are in a large block. The exterior walls can be covered with roofing tarpaulin, but in time it will pull away and will require constant repair or even complete replacing.

Another problem connected with outdoor housing is cleanliness. The area directly in front of the hutches should be paved. This will assist in cleaning, as such a surface can be washed down periodically. Food that is dropped onto the floor will quickly attract all kinds of vermin. Not only is this unhealthy for the rabbits and the rabbit fancier, but the neighbors will not be pleased either!

Only the very best materials should be used to construct outdoor housing. Wet weather will quickly take its toll on absorbent lumber or other unsuitable materials.

Many commercial rabbitries use wire pens instead of wooden hutches. These pens have the distinct advantage of not requiring any sort of bedding. The waste from the rabbits drops directly onto the ground, where it can be collected daily. Some fanciers breed worms in the accumulated excrement under the pens.

Wire pens are easy to make, they are inexpensive and will last for quite some time if they are maintained. The pen is made from a single piece of wire, preferably of 14 or 16 gauge. The back,

An arctic hare showing its brown fur which is present for the most part of the year except during winter. Hares and rabbits look alike and they are placed in the same family but some internal structural differences and different living and breeding behaviors set them apart.

A wild European rabbit. Its natural coloration blends well with the environment. This and its capacity to move fast enable it to survive in the wild. Some mammals living in the northern latitudes replace their colored fur with white during the winter months. Shown is an arctic hare in its winter pelage (below).

Hutches in commercial rabbitries usually have wire mesh floors; they are easy to clean and stay odor-free and damp-free. Note the feeder which can be filled from the outside.

sides and front are all made from this single piece of wire with the corners simply bent at right angles.

Half-inch by one-inch wire is most suitable for this purpose. Anything larger will be a hazard because the rabbits will be able to get their legs through the wire which will result in broken limbs.

An opening should be cut in the piece of wire that is to form the front of the hutch. This opening will form the hutch doorway. The door itself is made from another piece of wire the same size as the hole. The door is hinged with "C" clips applied with a special tool known as a C-clip pliers. The top and bottom of the pen are made from pieces of wire and fastened with C clips.

In the warmer areas in the United States, fanciers grow creeping plants around their pens to provide protection from the glaring rays of the sun. These plants must, of course, be harmless if eaten by the occupants of the pens. Another form of protection is canvas blinds that can be drawn when the need arises. These blinds can

also be used during cold nights when there is the possibility of frost. An increasingly popular method of constructing a frame for support of wire pens is the use of angle iron. One type of specially manufactured angle iron can be built in the same manner as a child's construction set. The pieces of iron have specially made holes that will take a nut and bolt at almost any angle.

When wire pens are used inside a building, there is no need for a frame. The wire pens are merely suspended from the ceiling with chains. Feeding rabbits housed in wire pens is a little different. The food has to be placed in receptacles that are fastened to the wire walls of the pen. Water has to be provided in either a gravity-fed bottle or an automatic watering system. Water pots are not practical because any spillage results in the soaking of the occupants in the pen underneath. Hay is provided in racks so that only a strand at a time can be pulled out by the rabbit as it browses.

A group of hares feeding. Notice the great similarity between them and the Belgian hare, a true rabbit.

A quartet of pet rabbits from Germany. These are Netherland dwarf rabbits; three self colored and one patterned.

A fenced outdoor accommodation for rabbits. For security the rabbits are kept in the individual hutches during the night and bad weather.

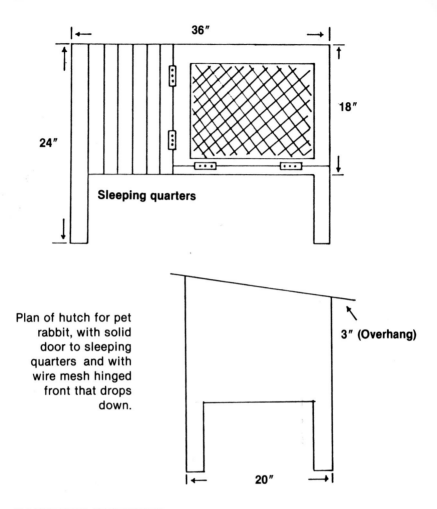

Plan of hutch for pet rabbit, with solid door to sleeping quarters and with wire mesh hinged front that drops down.

PAINTING HUTCHES

Painting has been touched upon in the preceding paragraphs, but it deserves special mention, as there is often confusion about materials and the correct method of application. The outside of the shed and hutches have to be able to endure the extremes of temperature and to counter the effects of wind and rain. The best, but perhaps the least decorative way of protecting the exterior of the shed is to coat it with creosote. Creosote is relatively cheap and can be obtained from most hardware stores. A drawback is the strong smell and fumes that it gives off. The smell and fumes will quickly fade away, but the rabbits must be removed from the premises while the creosote is being applied.

Enamel Paints

When enamel paint was first marketed, it contained a large amount of lead. In modern times, the use of lead in paint has largely been eliminated, and most types of enamel are considered safe for use on animal pens and houses. The outside of the rabbitry can be painted with any kind of gloss paint without any worry that the rabbits may come into contact with toxic properties. Although most modern paints do not contain lead, it is a good safeguard to use only paint that states on the label that it is safe to use in such circumstances.

The outside surfaces of the hutches can be painted with enamel, making them easier to wipe down and keep in good condition. However, extreme caution should be exercised on the inside of the hutches. Emulsion paint or the old-fashioned distemper can be used freely in these areas with complete safety. The great advantage of using emulsion paint inside the hutches is that it has little odor and it dries very quickly.

The interior of the rabbitry can also be treated with the creosote. However, all rabbits must be removed and cannot be returned to their quarters until the smell has subsided sufficiently for their safety. The choice of color depends on the fancier's personal preference. However, there is no color better than white to give a clean, hygienic effect throughout the interior of the rabbitry.

TRAVELLING BOXES

Travelling boxes are an essential part of the fancier's equipment. Without them, the transportation of his stock can be difficult.

Both the American Rabbit Breeders Association and the British Rabbit Council have drawn up standard sizes for boxes for each breed. The standard sizes refer to the weight and length of the groups of rabbit breeds. For example, Polish, dwarfs and some of the other smaller breeds are allocated a travelling box that will accommodate these miniature rabbits. Likewise, the larger breeds, such as the American, British and Flemish giants, must be carried in much larger travelling boxes. The genuine fancier will always have the welfare of his stock at heart and will make certain that his travelling boxes are of sufficient size to carry his stock with comfort.

The choice of a particular breed of rabbit for a pet must be given serious consideration. All bunnies are appealing, but a breed that will grow large may prove difficult to house and manage later.

Heavy tassels or tufts at the tip of the ears are very much desired in the English Angora rabbit by fanciers.

Travelling boxes for rabbits.

Many transport authorities will not carry livestock unless they are in approved containers. These containers must be large enough to accommodate the rabbit with comfort. If the journey is to be a long one, there must be provision for the animals to be fed en route. The box must be strong enough to withstand the rigors of handling while it is in transit.

All these basic requirements can be obtained from the offices of the travel agent.

There are also quarantine regulations to contend with; these rules must be strictly adhered to at all times. Shipping rabbits can be costly and time-consuming, but once all the details have been sorted out and the necessary documents obtained, the operation runs smoothly and efficiently. Most travel agents are only too pleased to see their charges safely and speedily on their way.

The fancier who breeds his rabbits solely for exhibition has to be able to provide his own transport to the various shows. The boxes in which his rabbits will travel should also meet basic requirements.

The fancier who has his own transportation has a distinct advantage over his counterpart who has to transport his stock by road or rail with an agent. The fancier who relies on such agents will necessarily be conscious of the financial aspect of this method of transporting his stock. The boxes in which his rabbits will travel must be light and very strong.

The shape and style of rabbit travelling boxes are more or less universal. These boxes can be purchased from fanciers who make them as a profitable sideline to their hobby. There is no reason why these boxes cannot be made at home from a few scraps of timber.

Opened travelling boxes showing the interior compartments for two and for three rabbits.

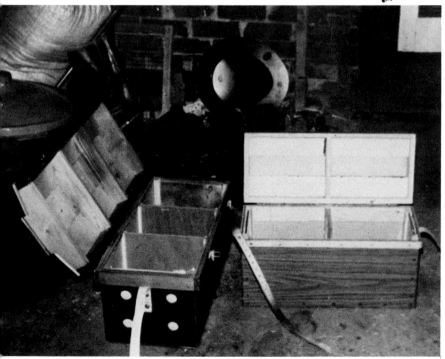

A chocolate brown English Angora rabbit.

A white English Angora rabbit. Regular grooming and clipping at least once a year will keep the fur in good condition.

A white French Angora rabbit. French Angoras are heavier than English Angoras and have less extensive tufting on the ears.

A colored French Angora rabbit.

Plywood is perhaps the best material to use, as it is light and strong. The plywood can either be varnished to show the natural beauty of the wood or it can be painted in a favorite color. For ease of handling, a strong leather strap should be fixed to each end so that it fastens with a buckle over the top of the box. Too much emphasis cannot be placed on the fact that the strap should be made of leather and that it be really strong. Cheap, thin straps will not last very long. A worn box strap can result in an accident and possibly the loss of a rabbit if the box should fall from any great height.

OTHER EQUIPMENT

To complete his set of equipment, all the fancier needs is a good sweeping brush and hand brush, as well as a strong shovel. These tools are invaluable when it comes to the regular routine of cleaning. To maintain cleanliness, the interior of each hutch must be cleaned out thoroughly. It is better to use good quality equipment that will do the job properly than to struggle with totally unsuitable tools.

Food And Feeding

There is some truth to the myth that rabbits will eat just about anything and that they can be fed on any old scraps from the kitchen. It is true that the domestic rabbit will eat as much greenfood as is placed before it, but that does not mean that the rabbit will be in perfect condition or that what it eats is the correct diet. If the rabbit fancier wants to succeed in breeding good, strong, healthy stock, he **must** feed his animals properly. Good feeding is the foundation upon which the fancier must build; without it, there is no chance for success.

The fanciers of bygone days had to be content with the foodstuffs available. They fed whole grains, roots, hay and as much leafy greenfood as they could gather. Mashes were sometimes made of vegetable scraps, grassmeal and bran. Although this method of feeding was wholesome, it was a tedious and time-consuming business.

The greatest revolution in the rabbit world came with the production of the rabbit pellet. This was the answer to the fancier's prayer—a complete rabbit diet rolled into a tiny hard pellet. The early rabbit pellet was basically grassmeal with added vitamins and minerals. After years of constant research, the modern rabbit pellet contains all of the above plus some roughage, animal proteins, milk fat and trace elements.

The nutritional requirements of the rabbit cannot be reduced to a formula, because the rabbit requires different amounts of each factor at different stages of its life. For example, does that are not breeding require less protein than does that are suckling young, and a doe that has a litter in the nest requires more protein, because she has to provide enough to feed her young and maintain her own body in good condition.

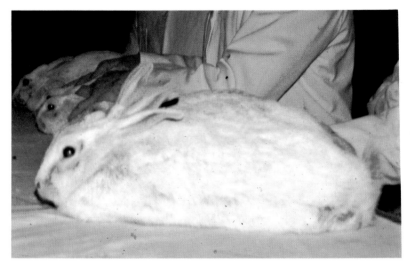

Several argente bleu rabbits on the judging table.

An argente de Champagne rabbit. The "old silver" appearance of this breed is caused by the combined effect of jet-black guard hairs interspersed between bluish white hairs.

Texas Agricultural Extension Service photo.

Argente creme rabbits. The rabbit in the upper photo was bred in the United States and that in the lower photo is from England.

Following is a table that provides a guide to the basic requirements of the rabbit at various stages of its life.

	Proteins	Fats	Fiber Roughage
Non-breeding does	10-15%	2-4%	20-30%
Breeding does	15-20%	3-5%	15-20%
Stud bucks	10-15%	2-4%	20-30%
Growing youngsters	10-15%	2-4%	20-30%

This table is only a rough guide, but it does give some idea of the differences in the diet during the different stages of rabbit growth. The protein-high foods include barley, oats, wheat, soya bean, linseed, milk and peanuts. These foods are also fatty, but the fat content is much lower than the protein content. The fibrous or roughage foods are found among the various hay types and roots such as carrots, turnips, and beets.

PROTEIN

The term protein is vague, as it refers only to the known group of amino acids which totals 23 nutrients. No one protein is exactly the same as another; each has a different role in feeding and maintaining the body in good condition. Basically, proteins are the foundations upon which the body is built. Protein is the main requirement for good growth. It is essential if the growth rate is to be kept at a constant level.

The quality of the proteins contained within the feed is very important. For example, if a feed of 20 percent protein is deficient in a number of amino acids, the growth rate of animals fed on it would be lower than of those fed on a feed that contains 15 percent protein but has a higher amino acid content.

It should be evident that lactating does and growing youngsters rely heavily on the proteins contained in the food they receive. If protein of the right type is not present in large quantities, the rabbit will be unable to maintain body growth. The breeding doe will be unable to maintain a high milk content to feed her youngsters.

CARBOHYDRATES

The main source of energy of living organisms is a group of organic compounds called carbohydrates. These compounds contain only carbon, oxygen and hydrogen. The basic carbohydrate molecules are the simple sugars that form more complex substances like the starches and cellulose. Plant materials contain cellulose and starches, and seeds are especially rich in starches. Animals are able to break down carbohydrates with specific enzymes during digestion, and the end products are stored in the body or burned during metabolism, releasing energy and some waste products (water and carbon dioxide).

FAT

Fatty substances like carbohydrates provide energy to the body, but unlike carbohydrates they may contain other elements (phosphorus and nitrogen) in addition to carbon, hydrogen and oxygen and they are not soluble in water. Excess carbohydrates are stored in the body in the form of fat and when needed fat is broken down during the process of movement and all other actions connected with everyday life.

An excess of fat results in the surplus fats being stored as extra weight. An example can be seen in the hibernation process of many animals. During the warmer seasons of the year, when food is plentiful, the animal eats until it becomes quite fat. When the colder weather comes, the animal goes to sleep. During this deep sleep the respiration is reduced, but energy is still needed to keep the body working, so the fat reserves are slowly used up. When spring arrives the animal is quite lean. Once more it will eat as much as it can in order to prepare for the next winter.

Although the rabbit does not hibernate, its excess fat is stored in the same way. Breeding does that are fat, and therefore not in breeding condition, do not readily mate; when they do mate, the chances of a litter being conceived are remote. Fat does also have difficulty parting with their young at birth.

FIBER

Crude fiber is found in the stems and the leaves of many plants. Fiber is really a non-digestible material, but it plays a vital role in the metabolism of the body.

Fiber which adds bulk to the feed is split into digestible and non-digestible fiber. In the rabbit, the non-digestible fiber is passed through the body in the form of fecal pellets. The digestible fiber is transformed by the rabbit's body from the non-digestible fiber and is retaken into the body during coprophagy.

The Belgian hare is not a hare but a true rabbit, despite its great resemblance to the wild hare. To maintain its trim appearance a Belgian hare should be exercised outside the hutch.

A brown hare. Unlike the true rabbit, hares are born with fur and are able to move soon after birth. Many of the species live in open grasslands and are mainly nocturnal.

Bulky foods have less feeding value; therefore, more of this type of food is required to provide the body with all the vital properties that it requires to maintain a good health. Hay is very rich in fiber, but some types of hay have more fiber content than others. Old hay will contain less digestible fiber than newly cut hay. Hay that is leafy has more feeding value than hay that is all stalks and stubble. Legume hay is hay gathered when the grain has been harvested. It is much richer in food value than hay made of normal grasses.

Rabbits will eat hay when they are off their normal feed of pellets and grain. Hay is therefore valuable during periods of excess heat when less food is being eaten by the rabbit. As a general guide, hay should be fed to rabbits at least once a week.

VITAMINS

Vitamins are essential for the development and maintenance of the body. Roughly speaking, the vitamins are divided into six main groups. Each is given a letter to denote its particular group.

VITAMIN A: The rabbit can manufacture its own vitamin A from fresh green food. Vitamin A, which is required by the rabbit for body growth, is also found in fish liver oils. Nervous stress has been attributed to a lack of vitamin A. It is also known that rabbits deficient in this vitamin are more susceptible to certain nervous disorders. Wry neck and other disorders that are accompanied by fits are blamed on the lack of vitamin A.

VITAMIN B: Vitamin B is found in fresh greenfood and is also made by the rabbit. This vitamin is crucial for bone growth and development. It is not usually added to rabbit food formulas.

VITAMIN D: Vitamin D has to be part of the animal's dietary supplement. It can be found in hay, but not in sufficient quantities to preclude adding the vitamin to the rabbit feed. Small amounts added to the feed promote calcium retention in the blood, which is necessary for good bone growth. Rabbits that are deprived of vitamin D can develop rickets.

VITAMIN E: Cereal grain, fresh greenfood and grain germ oil are all rich in vitamin E. If too much cod liver oil is added to the rabbit's diet, it will destroy all the vitamin E content of the feed, leaving the rabbit deficient in this important vitamin. Muscular dystrophy is caused by the lack of vitamin E; in serious cases the fertility of breeding does is affected.

VITAMIN K: Pelleted foods contain large amounts of vitamin K. It is important for skin growth and hair development. Mange and other skin disorders are a direct result of omitting vitamin K from the rabbit's diet.

FOODSTUFFS

In order to maintain rabbits in good health, the fancier will need to understand all the information provided about the nutritional requirement of his stock. He will also need to know what foodstuffs to feed in order to gain the best results.

Pellets

Pellets are perhaps the most popular of the present-day methods of feeding rabbits. Pellets are manufactured from high-quality ingredients and formulated to provide the rabbit with a balanced diet in one easy-to-prepare commodity.

Pellets can vary from batch to batch, and it is best to try to maintain a balance in feeding. Therefore, when feeding pellets as an exclusive diet, it is good to mix a new batch with a good portion of the last batch. The change from one pellet to another is therefore softened, and mild stomach disorders are avoided.

Pellets vary in color. Although they are usually some shade of green, some are very dark while others are light in color. The color will vary according to the manufacturer's specification. A good pellet is very hard and does not crumble easily when squeezed. Dust is unavoidable, but it should be kept to a minimum.

Pellets are easy to store and should be kept dry at all times. Hay should always be fed when pellets form the main part of the diet so that a constant level of roughage is maintained.

Oats

Oats have been used as a rabbit food for many years. They are rich in protein and have very good feeding value. Good quality oats are golden in color, and each load should contain a minimum of chaff or waste.

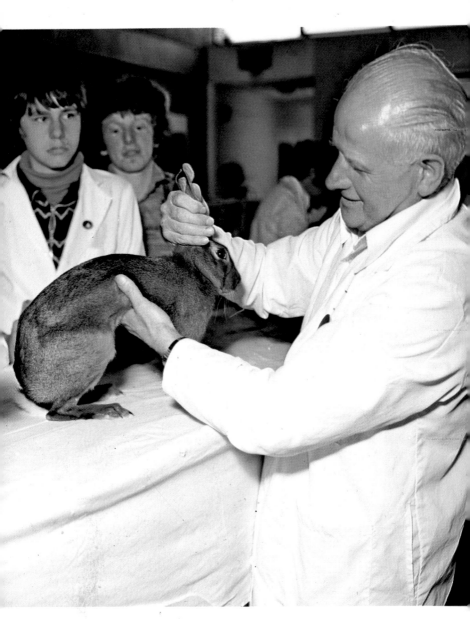

A Belgian hare being judged. Specimens of this breed should have a lanky body with long legs and ears. Only one color, a rich red of tan or chestnut shade, is acceptable. Entrants also should not weigh more than nine pounds.

A black American checkered giant. The standard for the checkered rabbit is specific with respect to the number, size and position of the markings. Besides black, blue markings are acceptable for this breed.

A blue Vienna rabbit. A good specimen could also be exhibited with other fur breeds.

While crushed oats are sometimes preferred to whole oats, crushed oats have a high waste content, and the rabbit can become very fussy about which part of the oats it will eat. Oats and pellets are a very popular combination as a rabbit diet in England and are fed to most exhibition rabbits.

Wheat

Wheat is also fed with oats in many rabbit diets. Wheat is very rich in vitamin E and contains a generous amount of crude protein. Too much wheat can induce excessive body heat. Continuing to feed wheat under these circumstances will make the food un-

Pelleted rabbit food comes in a variety of shapes, size and color. It is nutritionally complete, so that green foods are not necessary, although in some cases additional roughage should be given to prevent constipation.

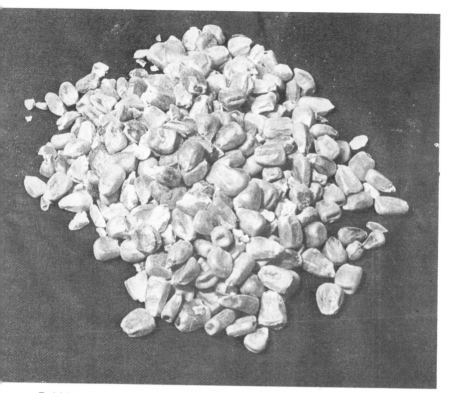

Rabbits also eat corn, which is cheap and easy to get, but rabbits cannot live on corn alone.

palatable to the rabbit. As with oats, the grain should be whole and of a good golden color with little chaff. The grain should be round and wholesome.

Barley

Barley is another good food for exhibition rabbits. It is very useful for building up the good hard flesh required in the Polish, silver and Belgian hare. Although it has slightly less feeding value than either oats or wheat, it is still a very useful food and can be added to the usual diet in small quantities.

Corn

Corn is rarely added to rabbit food, except inexpensive mixtures of pet food. Maize can often be found in poultry feed. When fed to rabbits, the corn is a very useful conditioner.

A white Beveren rabbit.

A blue Beveren rabbit. Black is the third color recognized; brown Beverens have been bred and are recognized in England.

A white Beveren rabbit exhibited in the United States.

A blue Beveren rabbit bred and shown in the United States.

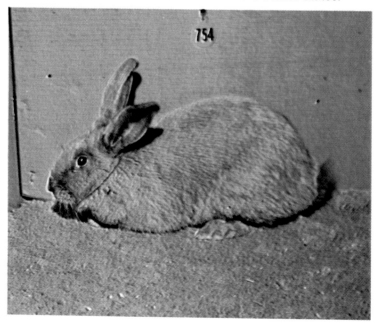

69

The large seeds in this pet food mixture are the sunflower seeds. Sunflower seeds contain oil so they are a good conditioning food during molting.

Sunflower Seed

Sunflower seed is not very often used by the rabbit fancier. However, because it heats the rabbit's body, it could be used to advantage during the molt or when a reluctant doe is to be brought into breeding condition. An excess of sunflower seed can cause overheating of the blood; therefore it should be used sparingly.

Linseed

Linseed can be used in the same dosages as sunflower seed. It is very oily and has a heating effect. For many years the use of linseed has been advocated as a molting aid. Although it has a laxative effect, it does give the coat an added sheen. For this reason, a cake made from linseed and bran can be fed to exhibition stock some weeks prior to an important show.

Bread

Dried bread is often fed to rabbits. When baked very hard it can be useful as a variation to the usual diet of pellets and oats. It will also provide the rabbit with something on which to exercise its teeth. Fresh bread should never be offered to rabbits, as it is unpalatable and will become soiled if left in the hutch for too long. Stale bread can be fed after it is baked in the oven. Bread containing mold should never be given to rabbits. Brown or wholemeal bread is of greater feeding value than white bread, as it contains much more wheat germ.

Greenfood

A wide selection of greenfood can be fed to rabbits. Although rabbits will always eat greenfood, it does not follow that the greenfood will do any real good if care is not used in its selection. In fact, the reverse is often the case. Poisoning can result from indiscriminate feeding of greenfood.

Basically there are two sources of greenfood—the foods that are cultivated in the garden and those that grow in the fields as wild plants. It is very important that all greenfood be washed thoroughly before it is offered to rabbits.

Many modern crops are sprayed with pesticides. Several species of animals and birds have been almost wiped out by the use of these pesticides. Even garden fertilizers can have harmful effects if they are used in large quantities. Therefore, the rabbit breeder should take great care in the choice and quality of all greenfood. After the greenfood is washed, the leaves should be inspected for any signs of disease or infestation by grubs or parasites. Young rabbits can be scoured easily if fed an excess of greenfood. The breeder should exercise caution in this direction.

The quality of greenfood depends greatly upon the time of year it is gathered. Plants that have gone to seed have less feeding value than those that are young and tender. The older a plant, the more woody the stems and leaves and the more fiber they will contain. Fibrous plants are difficult to digest, and much of the plant is wasted.

Some wild plants are useful as medicinal aids and can be grown in the fancier's garden for that purpose.

Although the number of root crops is restricted, they are very good food for rabbits of all ages. Among these roots are beets, turnips and carrots. Root crops should also be thoroughly washed and inspected for signs of disease and pests. Root crops are particularly susceptible to rot and anything that is infested should be discarded.

Cultivated Greenfoods

The rabbit fancier who has a small amount of land can grow some food especially for feeding to his stock. Most plants take up very little room and can even be grown among flower beds in the decorative garden.

A Californian rabbit.

The Californian is a fancy breed and a fur breed as well. Ideally, the useful parts of the pelt should be white; color should be confined to the extremities only.

The cinnamon is a breed recognized in the United States. Complete absence of markings (butterfly smut, dark extremities, eye circles) is a disqualification in the cinnamon.

A wild chinchilla. Chinchillas are highly prized because of their luxurious and beautiful soft fur. The chinchilla rabbit gets its name from this rodent.

LETTUCE: Lettuce is the most common greenfood that is regularly offered to rabbits. It is always welcomed by the stock and is a very good source of vitamins. It does not take up much room and can be accommodated in the flower bed of any garden. It could even be grown in a window box if earth suitable for growing plants is hard to find.

Any yellow or insect-infested leaves should be discarded and only the firm, healthy green leaves used as fodder. Lettuce should not be given to young rabbits until they are at least two months old, and even then it should be used with discretion.

CABBAGE: Another popular garden vegetable that is useful to the rabbit fancier but that can do untold harm if it is abused is cabbage.

Cabbage can be fed when scraps are available from the kitchen. Growing cabbage just for rabbits can take considerable space in the garden and the plant takes many months before it is ready to eat. Therefore, its cultivation is not really worthwhile. When all the leaves have been gathered and used, the cabbage stalk can be left in the ground, where it will grow new shoots. If the shoots are fed to the stock they make an excellent tidbit. The remaining stalk can then be chopped up into manageable pieces and fed to rabbits. The stalk will provide the rabbit with something on which to nibble.

An excess of cabbage will cause the rabbit's urine to smell strongly. If fed to young stock without being mixed with other greenfood or hay, cabbage can give them severe diarrhea. The use of other greens or hay will counteract the laxative effect to some extent. Yellow or diseased leaves should be discarded.

CHICORY: Chicory is perhaps the best of all cultivated greens that can be used by the rabbit fancier. It is a biennial that can be sown from seed with very good results. Chicory requires no special cultivation, as it will grow well in the poorest of soils. Its value as a conditoner has been noted for many years. Rabbits that are fed chicory regularly develop a sleek, glossy coat.

CAULIFLOWER: Cauliflower, like cabbage, takes up considerable space in the garden and is not really worthwhile to cultivate, but it is a safe and nutritious greenfood that can be fed to stock of all ages.

CLOVER: Clover is not as popular as its feeding value deserves. It is very nutritious and makes the very best hay when dried. Clover hay is prone to attacks of mildew and therefore should never be stored in a damp area.

KALE: Kale can be grown by a rabbit fancier with very limited garden space. It is a very useful plant and can be gathered at any time of the year. Once the plant reaches maturity, the outer leaves can be gathered periodically, which will encourage the appearance of new shoots. Sprouting kale is one of the most popular types. If the stems of this variety are left in the ground after all the leaves have been harvested, they will produce new shoots. The new shoots and part of the parent stem can be transplanted to start new plants. The remainder of the parent stalk can be cut up and fed to the rabbits.

PARSLEY: Parsley is an herb usually grown for use in the kitchen. It takes up very little room in the garden and is one of the best greenfoods for rabbits. This plant is a perennial and will last for many years if treated with care.

The outer leaves of parsley should be picked before they mature or they will become coarse and unpalatable. Because parsley has properties that have a stimulating effect on the rabbit's system, it should not be fed in excess. Parsley is often fed to stud bucks to bring them into top form. The plant can also be fed to breeding does with the same effect.

SPINACH: Spinach is a safe greenfood and should be fed to rabbits whenever the opportunity arises.

BRUSSELS SPROUTS: Like cabbage, Brussells sprouts should be fed with discretion, as they can make the rabbit's urine smell strongly. Brussels sprouts are very nourishing and may be fed as an alternative to the usual greenfood. Although the stalks are tough, they can also be fed to rabbits, which will enjoy the exercise for their teeth.

CARROTS: Carrots are the most common root crop fed to rabbits. They are very sweet and easily digested by stock of all ages. Carrots can be grown in the smallest of garden plots and require very little attention except for occasional weeding. But carrots are

A chinchilla rabbit, two years old.

A chinchilla rabbit. This is the standard type bred in England.

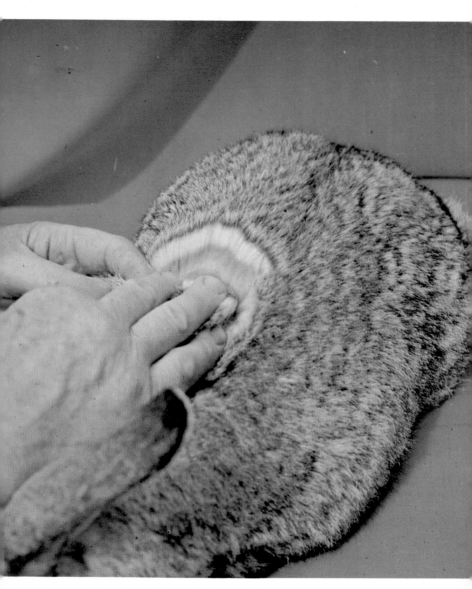

Fur of a chinchilla rabbit stroked back to show "pearling."

very cheap to buy at the market. Unless they can be grown in large quantities, their cultivation is not really profitable.

Young tender carrots are very palatable, but if they become stale they will be leathery and dry.

Carrot tops which are waste from the kitchen should be fed to rabbits whenever available.

SWEDES AND TURNIPS: Turnips and swedes (also called Swedish turnips and rutabagas) are root crops that can be fed at any time of the year. Quite a large amount of space is needed for their cultivation, but after harvesting the roots can be stored in an airy, dry shed for many months. When feeding swedes or turnips for the first time, it is advisable to add a small amount of hay, as the sudden change to these roots can result in stomach upsets. Leftover tops from the kitchen can be fed to stock of all ages at any time of the year.

RASPBERRY: The fruit of raspberry plants is often overlooked by the fancier. Raspberry has powerful astringent properties. If used in time, it will save the life of many a young rabbit that has scoured. The leaves and soft stems of raspberry are relished by all rabbits. The prickly thorns never seem to bother the rabbit at all.

Wild Plants

The fancier who has the welfare of his stock at heart should make a detailed study of the wild plants that grow in the neighborhood of his home.

Many wild plants have strong healing powers. The ability to use them will give the breeder of exhibition rabbits a head start over his less knowledgeable competitors. However, it goes without saying that a mistake can be deadly. In the use of wild plants, knowledge is the key. Do not feed anything that you cannot positively identify.

BRAMBLE: The bramble is the wild raspberry the was discussed under the heading of cultivated plants. When picking bramble, it is important to be certain that none of the leaves show signs of raspberry mosaic—a disease peculiar to the plant.

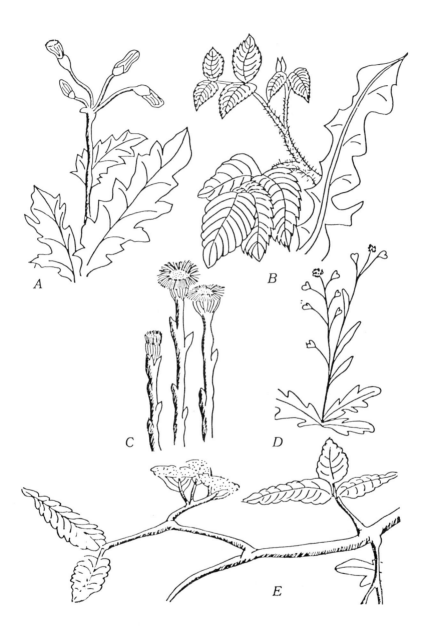

Safe or non-poisonous wild greenfoods. **A.** Groundsel (yellow),
B. Raspberry, **C.** Coltsfood (yellow), **D.** Shepherd's purse,
E. Ground elder (white).

An American chinchilla rabbit.

The chinchilla rabbit's fur must first of all be soft, dense and fine. Without the necessary texture, color will not be enough to satisfy a very discriminating and competitive fur industry.

Giant chinchilla rabbit. This American breed of chinchilla rabbit can weigh as much as 16 pounds.

The chinchilla giganta is the larger of the two chinchilla rabbit breeds in England.

SHEPHERD'S PURSE: Shepherd's purse is the most valuable wild plant that the rabbit fancier can feed to his stock. The powers of the shepherd's purse as a conditioner are well known. It is also one of the medicinal plants that will halt an attack of scours in its early stages. The plant grows about 18 inches to two feet high when mature and has long, slender stems from which the tiny heart-shaped leaves grow. The tiny white flowers grow in clusters. Shepherd's purse can be found growing on waste ground, especially on demolition sites.

DOCK: There are two useful types of dock, the broad-leafed dock and the curled dock. The broad-leafed dock has large, oval-shaped leaves of a leathery texture that lie flat along the ground. The curled dock is upright, with slender leaves that are slightly curled along their entire edge. This plant is useful when introducing young stock to greenfood for the first time, as it is slightly astringent. It should be mixed with a little freshly cut grass to make it more palatable. Plants that have gone to seed should be avoided, as the leaves lose much of their feeding value at this stage.

CHICKWEED: Chickweed can be found in almost every garden. No matter how meticulous the gardener is in his weeding, there is always at least one plant that manages to avoid the hoe.

The plant grows to a full height of about one foot, but most are eliminated by the gardener long before they reach this height. The small leaves are egg-shaped and grow in alternate pairs on a long, thin stem. The flowers are tiny and white. Chickweed is of very little feeding value, but it will be accepted by stock of all ages. Some authorities advocate its use during the molt.

COLTSFOOT: The flowers of the coltsfoot appear long before the umbrella-shaped leaves. The undersides of the leaves are covered with a silvery hairy down. The stem is scale-like; the flowers are yellow. Coltsfoot does not have any special powers, nor is it of any specific feeding value, but it is welcomed by all kinds of stock. It is most useful when mixed with other greens and served with other greenfoods.

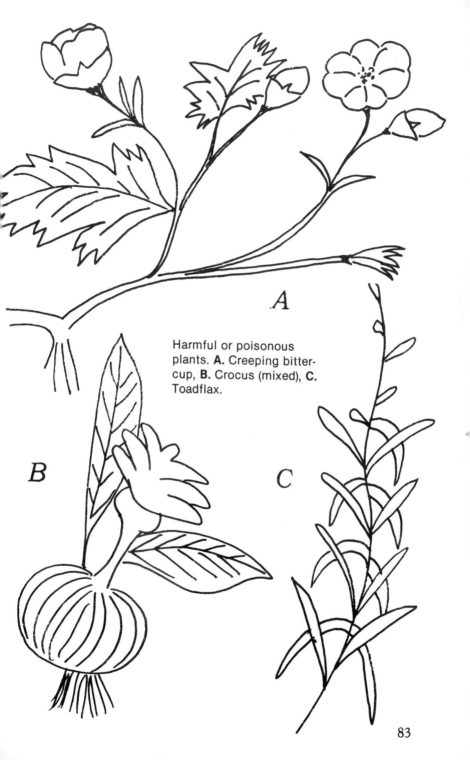

Harmful or poisonous plants. **A.** Creeping bittercup, **B.** Crocus (mixed), **C.** Toadflax.

A chinchilla rex rabbit.

A chinchilla rabbit with normal fur.

A standard chinchilla rabbit bred in the United States. It is not any different from the chinchilla recognized in England.

A chinchilla satin rabbit. The satin factor greatly improves the texture of the chinchilla coat.

DANDELION: Although dandelion is really a wild weed, it can be cultivated on any spare land for the sole purpose of feeding it to rabbits. The appearance needs little description, as the dandelion is known by almost everybody.

The long, sword-shaped leaves are serrated along the edges and fleshy in texture. The plant's hollow stem bears the bright yellow marigold-like flower. Dandelions are a tonic and very useful for cleansing the blood. If an excess of dandelion is fed to young stock, kidney damage could result.

GROUNDSEL: The tiny groundsel is another of the rabbit fancier's greatest friends. It has a slight laxative effect, but it also stimulates the molting rabbit. This is very useful when stock sticks in the molt.

A little groundsel should be fed to the molting rabbit every day until the desired effect is evident—a loosening of the coat and the falling away of the dead hairs. The plant is dark green, with clusters of tiny yellow flowers on a single stem. Although it grows only a few inches high, groundsel has a reputation as a nuisance to the serious gardener. The plant is very tenacious and will flower all year round if left undisturbed.

BINDWEED: The bindweed is often confused with poison ivy because the stems and leaves closely resemble those of the common ivy. There are two main plants of the bindweed family, the greater and lesser bindweed. The greater bindweed has pure white, bell-shaped flowers. It is often found rambling along fences in gardens that have been neglected. The lesser bindweed also has bell-shaped flowers, but they are striped mauve and white. This plant grows among corn plants and entwines itself among stalks of wheat and oats. The plants themselves are not really poisonous until they reach the seeding stage. At this time the lesser bindweed bears berries that are red to black in color.

FOXGLOVE: All varieties of foxgloves are poisonous and should never be fed to rabbits. The flowers are bell-shaped and pale blue in color. The plant is generally found growing along hedgerows and reaches a height of about three to four feet when mature.

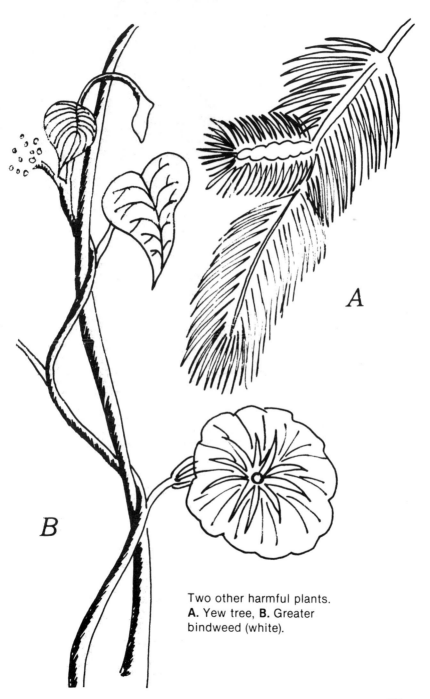

Two other harmful plants.
A. Yew tree, **B.** Greater
bindweed (white).

The Dutch is probably the most well known of the fancy rabbits. These are black Dutch; a younger specimen is shown above and an adult below.

A tortoiseshell Dutch rabbit.

A brown gray Dutch rabbit.

HEMLOCK: The hemlock is a tall plant that cannot be mistaken once identified. The thick stem is smooth and mottled red and green. The leaves have a distinctive white tooth at the extreme end. All parts of this plant are dangerous. If gathered with hay, the toxic effects are reduced somewhat once it has dried thoroughly.

WILD POPPIES: The poppy is well known for its effect on the bodies of both humans and animals. The poppy sap has been the cause of fits and hallucinations in those who have dared to eat it.

LABURNUM: The laburnum is a common tree that grows in many suburban gardens. The flowers hang down in bright yellow clusters and are unmistakable. All parts of the laburnum are dangerous, especially the seeds. Young children have become very ill by eating the seeds.

LARKSPUR: The larkspur is a common garden flower that requires little description. The tall flower spikes are usually blue.

LOBELIA: There are two types of lobelia—the common garden blue lobelia that is very popular as a border plant, and the trailing lobelia, which also has blue flowers. Some strains have white flowers. These, too, should be avoided. These two types of the same plant are very dangerous and should never be fed even if mixed with other greens.

PRIVET: The privet is the most common hedging shrub of all. The privet is best avoided as the leaves of this evergreen have a bitter, acrid taste.

YEW: The yew is another common hedging shrub that has well-known poisonous properties. Horses and cattle have reportedly died after eating the leaves of the yew.

RHUBARB: Controversial reports exist on the use of rhubarb as a greenfood. The leaves contain oxalic acid, which, if ingested in great quantities, could certainly cause rabbits harm. Some experts maintain that rhubarb can be eaten by rabbits without any ill effects. The plant is best avoided to be on the safe side.

A mixture of rabbit pellets and oats. Pellets can be mixed with any other kind of supplement desired.

POTATO: The leaves and stems of the potato are considered by some authorities to be poisonous. They are best left alone to be on the safe side. The potato tuber, when boiled, is perfectly safe and can be fed in mashes to which bran is added to dry it off.

PURCHASING FOODSTUFFS

The prime considerations when buying feeding material for rabbits are cost and quality. As for all products, cheaper brands exist that are inferior in quality to the dearer competitors made from superior-quality ingredients. Which one to choose is a matter that only the individual rabbit fancier can decide for himself.

As a general guide, grain is graded according to its quality when harvested. Pellets, on the other hand, can be controlled by the manufacturer; therefore the quality is usually consistent. The best pellets are made from top-quality foodstuffs; the cheaper pellets are made from the waste collected in the cornmill or inferior quality foodstuffs. Not everyone can afford to feed his stock the best, but an effort should be made to feed the best that the pocket will allow.

Facial markings in Dutch rabbits are seldom exactly alike. The standard is very specific with respect to the size, color and extent of the blaze or Dutch facial marking. A brown gray Dutch rabbit is shown (below).

A black Dutch rabbit. Any black hairs in the white areas are faulted.

Grooming the coat of an Angora is not enough to keep the coat in show condition unless the rabbit is given proper nutrition. When feeding, a heavy bowl (earthenware or metal) is better than a lightweight container that is easily upset.

Poor feeding will show in the condition and reproductive quality of a fancier's stock, so it is in the fancier's own interest to feed his stock well on good-quality food.

Rabbit food can be purchased either at the local pet store or direct from the mill. The pet store is always the best outlet. Buying from the mill may be an advantage if food is purchased in huge quantities. However, pet stores are reliable; they offer high-quality food and can be trusted to stand behind their products.

It also may be worthwhile to ask the pet store proprietor if he can supply rabbit food in larger-than-normal quantities at a lower price. Perhaps the fancier could offer young rabbits that do not meet his own particular requirements to be sold in the pet store. These rabbits, while inadequate for exhibition, could make excellent pets. This may be one method of keeping the cost of food at a minimum for his breeding stock.

94

STORING FOOD

No matter how high the quality of rabbit food, it will quickly deteriorate if it is stored inadequately. The greatest enemy is dampness. Food should always be stored in watertight, resealable containers. Special bins can be purchased, but an ordinary garbage can can be utilized just as easily. These receptacles can be made of metal or plastic. Plastic is lighter and will outlast metal, which may rust.

Mice and rats are attracted by the presence of grain and can become a problem. It is better to keep the food receptacle well away from the main rabbitry. Mice and rats carry disease. Once these pests have access to grain of any kind, they will quickly infect the whole load. A small tin that will hold 5 to 10 pounds of food will suffice for use inside the rabbitry for the average breeder. Even if a tin of this size has to be replenished every day, it is much better than leaving large amounts of food near the rabbit hutches to attract vermin. Rats can devour newborn baby rabbits. Because their very presence will cause many does to destroy their litters, utmost care must be taken to prevent rats in the rabbitry.

Suitable containers for rabbit food. Food must not be left in uncovered containers (boxes, sacks and bags) to attract vermin. Dampness can also ruin good food and make it unfit for feeding.

95

A litter of Dutch rabbits. Note the variation in markings as well as in the colors.

In the blue Dutch rabbit the blue areas must be as dark as possible with lustre and without stray white hairs.

The unusual color of the yellow Dutch rabbit makes this variety more in demand now.

FEEDING VESSELS AND APPLIANCES

For the fancier who keeps only a limited number of rabbits, the earthenware bowl is perhaps the best receptacle in which to place the rabbit's daily rations. If the stock is fed the right amount of food, the earthenware bowl should be empty within half an hour, so the chance of the foods becoming soiled is slight.

Hoppers can be used if preferred. One type hangs on the wire of the hutch door; another is free-standing. The contents of the hopper can still be spilled by the rabbit, but it is a much more difficult task.

The automatic hopper is a large fixture that is constantly kept full, ensuring that the rabbits have food before them all day long. This type of hopper is more commonly used on the big commercial rabbit farms. As the rabbit eats from the bottom of the hopper, the contents fall down gradually, keeping the tray full all the time.

WATER AND WATERING SYSTEMS

The domestic rabbit must have fresh water available at all times. The type of vessel used is a matter of personal preference but the water must be fresh and clean. An adult rabbit of the larger breeds will drink at least one pint of water every day and sometimes even more. The smaller breeds will drink about two thirds of a pint of water a day. But rabbits differ in the exact amount of water that they will consume.

Water should always be offered fresh, and the vessels should be emptied and replenished daily whether the contents have been consumed or not. Stagnant water is a breeding ground for many harmful organisms. A plentiful supply of water should always be available to growing young stock and suckling does. Without water, the doe will have difficulty producing good quality milk on which to rear her litter. Even when a rabbit is off its food, it will always drink water.

There are many kinds of watering vessels and systems at the fancier's disposal. The most common method is the gravity-fed bottle. This is a glass or plastic bottle with a cork or a rubber stopper inserted into it. The bottle has a screw on top containing a metal or glass tube. The end of the tube is rounded off to inhibit the flow of water. Some models have a ball-bearing mechanism

Gravity-fed bottles for rabbits should have strong spouts; weak materials are easily broken or chewed. Three types of earthenware feeding vessels or pots (below).

A steel gray Dutch rabbit.

A gray Dutch rabbit.

A blue Dutch rabbit.

A chocolate Dutch rabbit.

A tri-color Dutch rabbit. The harlequin and the Dutch markings are combined in this complicated and not-too-easy-to-breed variety.

which restricts the flow of water until the animal drinks some of the contents.

When the bottle is inverted, a vacuum is created and the water will not run because of the device at the tube's tip. The rabbit can drink quite easily from the end of the tube without soiling the interior of the hutch. These bottles can be purchased at pet stores.

This is the most convenient method for the fancier with only a limited number of stock. However, these bottles are not without their drawbacks. Occasionally the metal tubes are soft and are easily punctured by the rabbit's teeth. If the bottle is dropped, it will break easily. If it is plastic, it can split along the molding seam. If the tube is punctured, the vacuum will be destroyed and the contents will run out. Some models have stainless steel tubes, which helps prevent the rabbits from chewing the metal.

If sawdust or bedding is piled against the end of the tube, a capillary action takes place and the water is drained into the bedding, leaving the rabbit thirsty and sitting on damp bedding. This type of accident can be prevented by placing the bottle higher up on the hutch front. The bottle is held in place on the front of the hutch by an elastic band and two hooks. The tube is pushed through the wire mesh so that the rabbit can reach the nozzle.

The old-fashioned water bowl is still used by many rabbit fanciers. However, it is not easy to persuade the rabbit that the water is for drinking and not for emptying all over the hutch floor! Heavier bowls can be used, but they too will be soiled by the rabbit as it quickly fills the pot with sawdust.

Another method of providing water is to use the inverted bottle on a different principle. A special device can be purchased that fits the neck of any large bottle. The apparatus includes a container. After fitting the device, the whole thing is turned upside down, including the bottle. The water runs into the container until it is full. The neck of the bottle rests just above the bottom of the container, creating a vacuum. No more water will run into the container until the rabbit has consumed some from the base.

The most competent and modern method of watering is the automatic watering system. Although it is undoubtedly the most expensive way of watering rabbits, once the unit is installed it is a permanent fixture that will last many years. Most commercial rabbitries use an automatic watering system because it saves time and

Hutch with drinking bottle attached to the front of wire doors.

effort. The basic principle is the same as the gravity-fed bottle. The bulk of the water is contained in a header tank or plastic barrel above the level of the hutches. The water is fed through plastic tubes along a row of hutches. At each hutch is a small branch from the main pipes. The branch has a rounded tip, as do the tubes on the bottle. Because a vacuum is created in the same way as the bottle, the water will not run out, yet it is available to the rabbits 24 hours a day. The tank or barrel must always be kept full.

The automatic system should be thoroughly cleaned out by flushing it regularly with a mild antiseptic and fungicide. Special preparations can be purchased for this purpose.

One fo the oldest of the fancy breeds, the English or English spot is an established favorite as a show and pet rabbit. For exhibition the position, number and shape of the markings are very important. This black English is posed so that almost all of the markings are visible.

In pet rabbits the position and shape of the markings or the color of rabbits are unimportant. Just select the rabbit which is attractive to you, provided it is in healthy condition.

The Basics of Breeding

Rabbits are famous for their ability to reproduce in large numbers. In the wild state, the does have been known to produce as many as four or five litters a year. The number of litters born in a year depends upon the rabbit's environment. The survival of the young is also largely dependent on the amount of food available during their first year.

Young rabbits fall prey to foxes, weasels, birds and other animals; therefore, the numbers born must be in excess of those required to maintain the rabbit population. The rabbit fancier does not have to confront these problems. He restricts his does in the numbers of litters they will be allowed to rear in one year.

The domestic rabbit doe may be reluctant to breed satisfactorily, which can cause problems for the newcomer to rabbit raising. Rabbits will not breed unless they are in tip-top condition. Does that are mated in poor condition will rarely carry their litters full term; if they do, the young will probably be weak and puny.

A common misconception about breeding is the idea that all that is necessary is to put the buck and doe together and, presto, they will mate. If it were really that easy, the rabbit fancier would have no problems at all.

The buck must be in perfect condition if the best results are to be obtained. As a general rule, the doe should always be placed into the buck's hutch. Some does will not tolerate the presence of another rabbit in their hutch. Even though the doe is willing to mate, she may attack a buck who invades her privacy.

The very sight of a doe will excite a buck, and he will jump around his hutch in anticipation. Once the doe has been placed into his hutch, she will usually cower in a corner because she is unsure of herself in strange territory.

As the buck and doe come together, the buck will rub his chin over the doe's back and hindquarters. His action will stimulate the doe. If she is ready to mate, she will raise her tail as a signal to him. The buck will then mount the doe, and the mating follows.

The actual mating lasts only a few seconds. When it is over, the buck will emit a stifled scream and fall from the doe. This is quite natural and need not cause concern to the newcomer to rabbit breeding. Some say that the buck screams as a direct result of pain, but this has never been proven conclusively.

The scream is an indication to the fancier that a mating has taken place. If the male and female are left together for about ten more minutes, the act will be repeated. This improves the doe's chances of conceiving and producing a litter.

It is always better to observe a mating than to leave the rabbits to their own devices. An over-eager buck could easily injure a doe. Some fanciers leave the doe with the buck overnight in hope that they will mate. This may result in wasted time, as it will be some time before the fancier has an indication that the mating has taken place at all.

When the handler is sure that a successful mating has taken place, he should gently remove the doe. Some breeders hold the doe stomach-side up when putting her back into her own hutch so that any sperm in the region of the doe's vagina will not be lost. There is not really any need for such extreme measures, as the sperm should already be on their way to meet the as-yet unfertilized eggs.

Once the doe is mated and put back into her own hutch, she should be left alone for a while to keep her quiet and restful.

TEST MATING

There are differing opinions as to the correct time to test-mate a doe. Some experienced breeders say it should be done after 10 days; others say seven days later is the right time. Whichever time is chosen, the result should always be the same. If the doe is in fact pregnant, she will refuse to mate again. It should be apparent within a few minutes after putting the doe back with the buck whether she is going to mate.

A black English rabbit or an English spot, as it is known in the United States. The breed is available in several colors besides the black.

A blue English spot.

A chocolate English spot.

A gray English spot.

A gold English spot.

A lilac English spot.

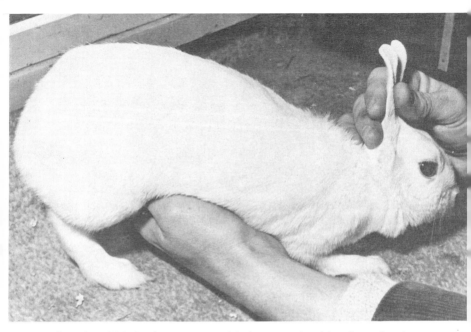

A female rabbit in the process of being examined by the palpation method to determine if she is pregnant.

If she refuses to have anything to do with the buck, he may attack her, so she should be removed immediately. On odd occasions the doe may attack the buck.

PALPATION

Palpation is a method of determining whether the doe is pregnant. Successful palpation is an art that can be acquired only with practice. At fourteen days after mating, the embryos will be large enough to be felt by hand.

The doe should be put on a suitable bench, with her ears held in the right hand. The left hand is slipped underneath her stomach. The doe should be very relaxed if the operation is to be done properly the first time.

The fingers of the left hand probe along the stomach towards the rear end of the doe. The developing embryos will be felt as a chain of marble-sized balls. Practice is needed to be able to find the embryos and confirm their presence.

PSEUDO-PREGNANCY

Pseudo-pregnancy is not peculiar to rabbits; many species of birds also perform this ritual. However, the unfertilized doe will take on the appearance of a pregnant doe, even to the extent of having swollen mammary glands.

At about the eighteenth day, the pseudo-pregnant doe will pluck fur from her chest and proceed to make a nest. This may go on for a number of days until it is apparent to the doe that no litter is forthcoming. At this stage the doe is highly fertile and should be mated again without delay.

THE STUD BUCK

In the well-run rabbitry, the stud buck is perhaps the most important rabbit of all. He is the pinnacle of the entire stud, and through him the quality of the herd is maintained.

In the world of exhibition rabbit, the stud buck is often a champion. However, this is not always true, as some very good stud bucks never make decent exhibition rabbits themselves. But in the breeding pen these bucks will never be surpassed.

The stud buck should be kept in first-class condition at all times. As his energy is needed to serve the does in the rabbitry, he should be fed the very best of foods in ample quantities. The stud buck should never be too fat or too thin.

A good stud buck will mate two or three does a week without any ill effects. More matings than this will reduce the buck's vigor and make him less competent.

THE CARE OF THE DOE AND YOUNG

Once it is established that the doe is pregnant, she should be looked after carefully. This does not mean that she should be wrapped in cotton wool and protected from everything. However, there are certain precautions the fancier should take. Noise from outside the rabbitry should be kept to a minimum. This is a precaution to prevent the doe from panicking, injuring herself and losing her unborn litter. The doe should be made as comfortable as possible in the hutch that she will litter. She will not show any obvious signs of being pregnant at first. About the twentieth day

A tortoiseshell English spot.

A tortoiseshell English rabbit. This specimen was exhibited and bred in England.

A sandy colored Flemish giant rabbit. Flemish giants are large rabbits; individuals can weigh as much as 20 pounds.

A light gray Flemish giant.

A litter of one day-old rabbits in a nest of hay and fur.

of her pregnancy, a marked increase in the size of the doe's abdomen will be noticeable. This is a certain indication that all is progressing well.

On the twenty-fifth day, the whole hutch should be cleaned out, and a liberal supply of fresh sawdust should be sprinkled all over the hutch floor. After the hutch is prepared in this manner, a nest box should be provided. Many types of nest boxes are available. The best is a wooden one with one side open. The nest box should also be lined with sawdust; a handful of hay should be added. Because some does will eat the hay, the fancier should keep an eye on the amount in the box and replenish it if necessary. The doe should be kept well supplied right up until the litter is born.

The gestation period of the rabbit is between 28 and 31 days. Most litters are born about the twenty-eighth day, but some does have been known to carry their young for as long as 35 days. These exceptions are rare but have been known to happen. As the time approaches for the doe to give birth, she may appear agitated and pace up and down her hutch front. She may even turn bad-tempered and try to bite the hand that feeds her. This behavior is quite natural and should not cause concern.

Most litters are born during the night or early hours of the morning. A certain indication that the litter is about to arrive is when the doe begins to pull fur from her chest to line the nest box. She may spend hours moving around the hutch with a mouthful of fur and hay. The doe will not build a nest as such but will be very intent on what she is doing. At this time the box must never be touched or moved. The litter will be born that night. The next day all action will have ceased, and the doe will sit on a corner of her hutch quietly munching at her hay. The nest box will be piled high with hay; on top of it will be the pile of fur from her body.

Before inspecting the litter, the fancier should move the doe to an empty hutch. It is very important that the human scent should not be detected by the doe on her return to the nest box. Before touching the nest box, the hands should be rubbed in some sawdust from a corner of the hutch that is used as the doe's toilet. This is not a pleasant task, but it is vital. Then, carefully part the fur on the top of the nest, taking great care not to touch any of the babies. A quick count will determine the number of young in the litter. If the variety is marked, it will give the fancier some idea of the quality of the litter as a whole.

Experienced fanciers will take this opportunity to remove any badly mismarked youngsters. If they are left in the nest, they will become another mouth for the doe to feed. Unless the fancier has an outlet for such wasters, it is better to cull them at this stage rather than to let them become an added burden on the doe with a large litter. Dead or stillborn young and weaklings also should be removed. Weaklings are best weeded out at this time, as they rarely mature into decent adult rabbits. (The breeder of the smaller breeds may keep these weaklings as they can later be bred to produce even smaller rabbits.)

The fur should be gently returned to its former position over the young. The fancier may notice that the youngsters actually lie on the nest box floor rather than in any kind of nest.

A black Flemish giant.

A blue Flemish giant.

A steel gray Flemish giant.

A fawn Flemish giant

A family of New Zealand whites. Commercial breeders usually keep one buck for every five or six does in their stud.

Maiden does are sometimes a little bewildered by all the confusion concerned with the birth of their first litter. These does will sometimes kick the litter all over the hutch and become indifferent to the fate of their young. This is known as a "scattered litter," a term commonly used within the fancy to denote the loss of a litter. If the young are not dead, they can be gathered up and warmed in the hand until they begin to move about. The nest can be put back into some kind of order and the youngsters returned to it. The doe should be taken out of the hutch for a short while to allow the youngsters to settle and warm each other with the heat from their own bodies.

Baby rabbits are not brooded by the doe at all. They keep each other warm with the help of the nesting material. Baby rabbits are born naked but quickly develop a fuzzy fur which helps further in keeping them warm.

After the litter has become settled and warm, the doe can be returned, but she should be watched carefully. Should she scoop out the nest again, little can be done. The young will have very little chance of surviving if left to their own devices. Neglected litters of young rabbits usually die during the night from exposure, and there is nothing the fancier can do about it.

It is a difficult task to hand-rear a litter of very young baby rabbits. Such small creatures require rich milk and have to be fed regularly every two or three hours around the clock. For the fancier who wants to attempt this task, powdered baby milk is the best substitute for the doe's milk. If it is unavailable, use one of the products designed for the feeding of newborn puppies.

On the other hand, if the doe seems less nervous and leaves the nest and youngsters alone after being returned to the nest box, there is a good chance that she will rear them without any further trouble. The female rabbit feeds her young only at night.

If things seem to be going well, the nervous doe should be left strictly alone. Any further intrusions will only induce her to scatter the litter once more. It is sufficient to watch the nesting material move to know that all is well within the nest box.

Any young that stray out of the nest box will die if they are not found in time. Those that survive long enough to be found can be popped back into the nest box without any fuss.

A white Flemish giant.

A Flemish giant rabbit from England.

The Florida white rabbit was developed mainly for use in research. It is a compact and medium-size breed, about four to six pounds in weight.

A black fox rabbit. In this breed the silver-tipped guard hairs on the side of the body are considered beautiful, and the entrant is not penalized.

Young that die during the night will be buried in the sawdust in the nest box—your nose will tell you where they are. Although these casualties will have to be removed, further disturbances should be kept to an absolute minimum.

Although the young rabbits will still be very small, they will be very active and they will crawl about the nest within a few days of birth. After three days, the young rabbits will be covered with a fuzzy, down-like fur. This is the first coat; it helps considerably to keep the young warm during the long, cold nights.

Day by day the youngsters will increase in size. They will begin to look more like rabbits as the ears unfold and begin to take shape. By the time they are ten days old, the young rabbits will be perfect miniatures of their parents. The eyes will still be shut tightly, but the limbs will be much stronger, and the baby rabbits will be able to move about much more easily. The doe should be fed double her normal rations at this time, because she will need all the nourishment she can get in order to feed her growing family.

At three weeks, the youngsters will begin to open their eyes. They often open one eye first and may remain one-eyed for a day or two. It is at this time that the litter will take its first tentative look at the outside world. Venturing from the nest box, they will inspect all the corners of the hutch, scampering back to the nest box at the slightest sign of danger.

This is a fine opportunity for the fancier to look at each youngster in detail, noting which ones look as though they will make the grade on the showbench. Only experience will help the novice determine which youngsters are worth keeping.

The young rabbits will have ferocious appetites at this age and the rations of the doe will have to be increased accordingly.

As they grow older, the rabbits will spend the greater part of the day outside the nest box, returning to it when night falls.

WEANING AND PUBERTY

From four weeks of age, the young rabbits will gradually be weaned by the doe. Her milk supply will gradually diminish, and the young will begin to nibble at the doe's solid food.

At first the young appear awkward when they eat, but they soon get the idea and look forward to feeding time. At this time a liberal supply of hay is a must. This helps the young to learn how to eat and also keeps their stomachs active between meals. No other special food should be offered to the doe or her litter. They will be quite content with the normal ration of pellets.

A gradual weight loss will be evident in the baby rabbits as they are being weaned. This is a natural loss of baby fat and is quite common.

When the litter is between six and ten weeks old, it can be separated from the doe. It is better to move the doe to a new hutch than to move the youngsters. The young rabbits will not miss the doe, as they will now be able to feed and look after themselves.

The age of sexual maturity depends largely on the size of the breed. Smaller rabbits usually reach sexual maturity at about three to four months, while the larger breeds do not reach this stage until they are five or six months old.

By this time the young should have been sorted out. Those that are to be kept for breeding or showing should be given a hutch of their own. The remaining youngsters will be either sold or culled.

Immature attempts at mating will occur if the youngsters are allowed to remain together after they have reached sexual maturity. These matings are usually infertile, but there is an odd chance that a litter will be conceived. Therefore, it is preferable to avoid possible mishaps.

Young rabbits should not be mated seriously until they are at least a month older than the stage of sexual maturity. In the smaller breeds this will be about five months old; in the larger breeds about seven months. First matings are often unsuccessful; with a little more experience, the young buck's testicles will descend properly and there should be no further trouble.

SELECTION FOR BREEDING

The best exhibition rabbits do not always make the best breeders. The breeder must reach a compromise whereby he selects the best available buck with the characteristics he requires.

The doe need not be the size required by the exhibition standard. She will be a better breeding doe if she is larger than normal, as she will be much stronger and better able to withstand the rigors of rearing a litter.

A lilac harlequin. Dove gray and golden fawn patches are present.

A black harlequin rabbit. In good harlequins the head is divided equally into black and orange colors. It is a difficult pattern to produce.

124

A chocolate harlequin. The colors that must be present are dark chocolate and the golden orange.

A black magpie harlequin. Note the pattern of the face; one side is black, the other side white.

An entrant is judged along with its peers (a class of Himalayans is shown).

Breeding can be very tricky. The wise breeder will observe that the rabbit that possesses the particular characteristic he wants to duplicate will also possess negative traits. Along with the assets are bound to be faults. If the faults are not monitored carefully, they will become a permanent feature of the strain.

To illustrate this, the case of a strain of self-black rabbits can be used as an example. Perhaps the stud buck has a good coat and excellent type. He may, however, carry one or two white hairs in his otherwise jet-black coat. The doe's coat may be slightly inferior to the buck's, but she may be of excellent type. She may have a far superior eye to the buck. Perhaps her biggest fault is that she, too, has one or two white hairs in her coat and a white patch under the soles of her feet.

The litter resulting from a mating between these two rabbits may produce a number of young who, like their parents, have good coats. But they may have the white hairs found in both the buck and the doe. Perhaps the white hairs will not be as pronounced, but they will exist. There may be a youngster in this litter that does not have as many good qualities as its brothers and sisters. However, it may be free from the white hairs that plague the rest of the litter.

This is the youngster to keep and to breed back into the strain, keeping an eye on the good characteristics that are developing in the gradual improvement of the strain. Any rabbits in new litters

A removable nest box filled with bedding. It is portable and easy to clean.

that carry the white hair fault should be eliminated. Thus the fault will gradually be bred out.

It may take years to completely eradicate the fault, and even then it may make an occasional appearance. But very gradually the breeder will reach the final stage where all the rabbits have improved in appearance and the white hair fault will be removed completely.

Selection for breeding is a precarious and difficult business, but it deserves the breeder's constant attention if the quality of the strain is to be maintained at a constant level.

In addition to good show qualities, other factors must be taken into consideration. One example is a strain of rabbits that are bad breeders. This fault can be diminished if the best mothers are selected from among the breeding does. All the poor mothers should be rejected unless they are of exceptional quality and considered useful for improving the show qualities or the strain in general. Very often the use of foster does will be helpful in this case.

A chocolate Havana rabbit. A rich chocolate brown color like that of the famous Havana cigar is required by the standard.

Uniformity of color is important in the Havana. White hairs and white toenails are faulted in show specimens.

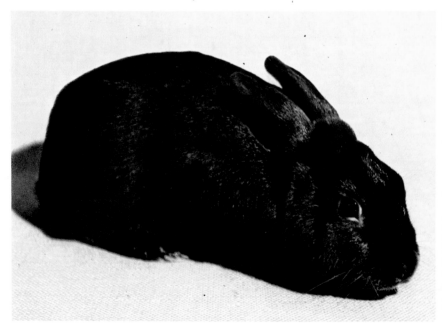

128

A blue Havana rabbit. This variety was first produced in the United States. The surface color is medium dark blue.

A black Himalayan rabbit.

The Role of Genetics

Genetics is the study of heredity. According to the dictionary, genetics is "the tendency of like to beget like." Genetics explains the factors that enable the rabbit to pass on the familiar characteristics of its species.

For rabbit breeders, the purpose of studying genetics is to produce better rabbits. This is achieved by selecting the best rabbits for breeding and discarding the worst and sometimes by crossing different breeds to produce the best features of both. Some of the basic methods of breeding that employ a knowledge of genetics are inbreeding, where close relatives are mated; linebreeding, where all progeny can be traced back to a common ancestor; and selective outcrossing, where rabbits that are not related are mated.

The basic hereditary characteristics of the rabbit are evident; they include ear length, coat quality and the rabbit's general appearance and body type. In addition to the characteristics that are visible in each rabbit are the hidden characteristics. For example, a black rabbit is obviously black. However, he also carries unseen traits that may show up in his offspring. Some hidden factors appear only rarely in the offspring.

If the rabbit fancier familiarizes himself with the fundamentals of genetics, he will be able to determine to a great extent the way his stock progresses. Improvement within a particular breed will be easier to attain, and time and money will be saved. Please note that the study of genetics is very complicated, and here we are covering only the barest of fundamentals.

A young rabbit receives its external characteristics from both its parents. The egg of the female and the sperm of the male each carries a nucleus. Within the nucleus there are tiny bodies called chromosomes. The chromosomes, which in rabbits number 22, are elongated in appearance.

The chromosomes contain a number of smaller bodies called genes. The genes possessed by any given rabbit govern both the physical appearance (the phenotype) of the animal and the genetic makeup (the genotype) that it is able to transmit to its own offspring. Each gene may govern one particular physical characteristic or a number of characteristics. Since each parent contributes chromosomes to the offspring, each parent consequently contributes genes.

Geneticists have assigned letters to the various genes as a means of identification. If the gene is dominant (that is, if it "suppresses" other genes governing the same characteristic) it is given a capital letter to identify it as such. Recessive genes (that is, those that are suppressed in the presence of dominant genes) are given a lower case letter.

The genes that dictate the coat color are often used when discussing genetics in general.

The following table provides the gene letter and the coat type or color that each letter controls:

TYPE OF COAT	GENE SYMBOL	
Agouti	A	The Agouti pattern.
	At	Tan pattern.
	a	Self color.
Black	B	Black color.
	b	Brown color.
Dilution	D	Dense color.
	d	Dilute color.
Color	C	Full color.
	cchd	Dark chinchillation.
	cchm	Medium chinchillation.
	cchl	Light chinchillation.
	ch	Himalayan color.
	c	Complete albinoism.
Extension of Black	Ed	Dominant black.
	E	Black as found in agouti.
	ej	Harlequin pattern.
	e	Black as found in yellows and tort.

Notice the strong resemblance of the head markings of this Californian rabbit to those of the Himalayan. However, the Californian is a large rabbit, about twice the weight of the Himalayan. A typical Himalayan rabbit (below) is small and sleek, never big or bulky.

According to the standard the Himalayans must have bright pink eyes. Cobbiness is also penalized in the breed.

Vienna White	V......................Normal color.
	v...............Blue-eyed white rabbit.
English Spotting	En...................English Spotting.
	en.......................No spotting.
Dutch pattern	Du.....................No markings.
	du....................Dutch markings.
	duw..................Dutch markings.
	dud..................Dutch markings.
Wide Band	W........Normal agouti band of yellow.
	w.......Yellow band wider than normal.
Rex Coat	R......................Normal coat.
	r..........................Rex coat.
	R2.....................Normal Coat.
	r2........Rex coat 2 (German short hair).
	R3.....................Normal Coat.
	r3........Rex coat 3 (Normandy rex coat).
Angora coat	L......................Normal coat.
	l...........Angora coat or long haired.
Satin coat	Sa.....................Normal coat.
	sa........................Satin coat.
Waved coat	Wa.....................Normal coat.
	wa.......................Waved coat.

From the above table it will be evident that the genes that control coat character and not color are all recessive.

In addition to this list are letters that denote abnormalities in the genetic make-up. The mutant gene for color will produce a color slightly different from that of the normal gene color. Sometimes the original gene will mutate further; the letter is then given a number to identify it as such a gene.

An individual rabbit can carry only one pair of genes of each particular type. Therefore, the genetic symbol would be either AA, Aa, Aat, atat, ata or aa.

In addition to these genes are a number of genes known as modifying genes. These genes are responsible for establishing the degree of shade obtained by the genes that will dictate the actual color. For example, a rabbit may be blue, red or yellow. But in one such litter from each color, there will be a distinct variation in the color of each individual.

In the same way, these modifying genes act upon other characteristics such as the ability of the doe to successfully rear a litter, the coat quality, the type, etc. But these genes act independently of the genes that control coat color, so it does not follow, for example, that they will produce females of a certain color that will always turn out to be bad mothers.

Some species of animals have genes that act collectively, that are "linked." This is particularly true in sex linkage, where a given trait is linked to the sex of the animal. In other words, a fancier can tell by the color of a certain animal which sex it is. Sex linkage in the rabbit is as yet unrecorded.

The genes that control the sex of the embryo are also passed on from each parent. But they are exact opposites and, unlike the other genes, do not make a pair. The buck carries an **X** chromosome and a **Y** chromosome. The doe carries two **X** chromosomes. If the **Y** chromosome of the buck pairs with the **X** chromosome of the female, the resulting embryo will have a pairing of **YX** and will be a male. If the other chromosome from the male—the **X**—pairs with the **X** chromosome of the female, the young rabbit will have a gene pairing of **XX** and be a female.

BREEDING FOR IMPROVEMENT

A knowledge of genetics is useful when the general standard of a herd or strain needs improvement. Genetics makes the work of improving a herd much easier. Yet the goals are never the same, even for fanciers who raise the same breed of rabbit. Each fancier has his own idea of what the perfect specimen should look like and which characteristic is of the greatest importance.

The fancier who breeds his stock for commercial purposes does not have the same problem. He knows what is required from his herd and will mate his rabbits with that aim in mind. For example, higher milk yield in the does may be the aim, or the growth rate of the young may require improvement.

Whether the fancier is an exhibition rabbit breeder or a commercial rabbit raiser, he must constantly seek to improve his stock.

The Himalayan markings have been bred in other breeds as the Netherland dwarf (left) and the Polish (below). However, the legs of this Polish rabbit are too pale in comparison to the ears and smut.

A lilac rabbit.

A lilac silver rabbit displayed at one of the rabbit shows in England.

The fancier who is at the pinnacle of success is just as vulnerable as the novice. Complacency sometimes creeps in when the experienced fancier thinks that further improvement is impossible. This is a dangerous state of mind, for even to remain in the same place in livestock breeding, one has to keep moving. The constant high quality of the strain has to be maintained.

If the fancier feels that he cannot improve his stock any further with the rabbits in his herd, he must seek rabbits from another strain that excel where his own stock is deficient. He will be able to further his aims and may even be able to add a few refinements.

Faults may be eradicated as soon as they appear. If faults are allowed to become established, they will be fixed within the stock and the fancier will have taken a long step backwards.

The experienced breeder may be able to discern with his eye which way his stock is progressing without the aid of the genetic system and its symbols. But the production of a mutant is a hit-and-miss affair. If the genetic symbols are recorded, it will be easier to reproduce a certain mutant than it would be if that mutant just appeared. In the latter instance, the breeder would have no idea how it came about and would lose much time in trying to find it again. He may even lose the new mutation altogether.

ENVIRONMENT AND INHERITANCE

The environment of a rabbit has a pronounced effect on the characteristics it inherits. Color is not affected by environment, because color is fixed by the genetic makeup of the rabbit at its conception. Other characteristics may be more directly affected by environment. Size is a good example. The potential size of bigger-than-normal individuals of given breeds is genetically determined, but of course the genetic trait for size can have its effects at least partially blocked through the influence of adverse environmental conditions. A rabbit may carry a gene for large size, but it won't get big if it's fed very poorly.

A fancier cannot hope to emulate the success of the breeder from whom he bought his stock if he does not manage his rabbits in the same superior manner. He may have the opportunity to breed rabbits equal to those of his successful predecessor, but the rabbits he breeds will never be given the chance to show their full potential if they receive insufficient nourishment and inferior housing. In time the all-around quality of the stock will deteriorate. Good housing and feeding may cost a bit more at the outset, but they will prove to be more economical in the long run.

INBREEDING AND LINEBREEDING

Inbreeding and linebreeding are two systems of breeding animals. Inbreeding is the mating of animals of close relationship. In linebreeding, one particular animal is selected as the common ancestor from which all the animals are descended.

Inbreeding

Inbreeding is a difficult science. Although it can be performed by the inexperienced breeder, it is usually not done in the same manner as the experienced breeder of livestock would do it. Because close relatives are mated, inbreeding will produce rabbits that all show the same characteristics. Each rabbit will look very much like the others.

Many fanciers are wary of inbreeding, because there are many pitfalls. In the same way that a good point can be fixed within the stock, so can a fault become a permanent feature. The breeder who plans to attempt inbreeding should remember that both faults and good points will become fixed. Once a fault is inbred, it is very difficult to eradicate.

Constant culling is an important aspect of inbreeding and must be practiced vigorously. A high standard of excellence must be constantly maintained. Any rabbit that falls below this standard must be culled. Just how closely related the rabbits are that are to be mated is a matter for the fancier's discretion. One fancier may consider the mating of brother and sister or father and daughter to be much too close and would prefer the mating of half-sister and half-brother or grandfather and granddaughter. Another may mate the brother and sister.

With inbreeding, of course, the desirable qualities of the stock are accentuated and the faults revealed, because the rabbits that are mated have nearly the same genes. If all the animals that display the faults carried by the undesirable genes are eliminated,

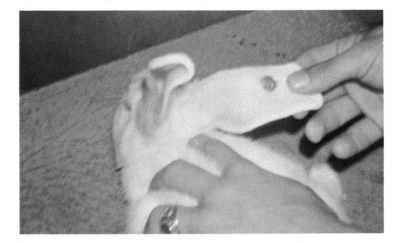

Upper photo: Some rabbit clubs accept only those rabbits bearing approved types of tattoos and will disqualify animals with unauthorized tatoos. Rabbits for laboratory use must have unmarked and unscarred ears also. Lower photo: If a lop rabbit's ears lack substance they are vulnerable to damage or injuries.

Contrary to popular beliefs a rabbit's ears are delicate structures. As seen in this photograph the ear is supplied with many thin-walled blood capillaries; rough handling can result in bruises, even hemorrhages at times.

141

the genes that carry the faults will eventually be eradicated. It is a slow and complicated process, but the rewards are well worth all the effort.

On the other hand, the rabbit fancier can be misled by the good qualities that his stock displays. He may become enthralled by the fact that the good qualities are evident in every rabbit he breeds. But he can be lulled into a false sense of security. For example, the breeder may be inbreeding rabbits that have beautiful coats. Because the coat quality has been inbred, all of the rabbits he produces may have really high-quality coats. In his excitement over the quality of their coats, the breeder may overlook the fact that a bad fault in his herd is eye color. If he does not work to eradicate this fault, it will ruin his herd.

The faults will always be there. If the breeder does not keep a sharp eye on them and cull those rabbits that possess them, the faults will become fixed within the stock. By this time it will be too late to rectify the faults, and the whole breeding plan will have to be started over.

Linebreeding

Linebreeding is perhaps the nearest the ordinary fancier ever comes to inbreeding. Linebreeding is practiced when a group, or sometimes even a single rabbit, is used as the head of a stud. All the rabbits in a line-bred stud can be traced back through their pedigree to a common ancestor. Each rabbit will be as closely related to the ancestor as the next.

SELECTIVE OUTCROSSING

The selective crossbreeding method is a rather haphazard system of breeding. It is the mating of rabbits that are pure in their respective pedigrees but in no way related. The choice of matings is often a matter of what one rabbit lacks that another can offer.

Selective outcrossing is used in the hope that the qualities of one or both rabbits will overcome the faults and failings of each particular rabbit. The aim is to produce a rabbit that is better all around than either of its parents. The desired result may sometimes be achieved, but only in the first generation. To maintain the good type, some inbreeding is essential. Inbreeding is necessary to fix the good qualities that are developed.

While a very good rabbit can be produced by selective outcrossing, there is no guarantee that good rabbits will be bred regularly.

If two rabbits from the first generation produced by outcrossing are mated together, the hidden faults that either or both carry will almost certainly become apparent. In fact, the offspring bred from this first generation mating will all be useless for exhibition. To eradicate these faults, inbreeding will be necessary, and very strict standards will have to be maintained.

In selective outcrossing, the hit-or-miss method often pays dividends when a winning combination is found. A certain buck with a certain doe may produce at least one youngster every year that will be very good. Winners can often be produced this way, but the superior young will not be produced as often or in such vast numbers as they would from inbreeding.

SELECTION AND CULLING

If the breeder of exhibition rabbits wants his stock to be the best there is, he will have to cull severely. This fact must be faced. It is not a pleasant idea; those who detest this practice will have to find another outlet for all the unwanted stock.

It is fine to say that culling must be severe and the more severe the better. Yet what will the breeder use as stock for future breeding? Breeding stock must possess as many good points as possible. The faults will still be there, of course, but they will have to be kept at a minimum. A line must be drawn somewhere between culling and keeping if the fancier is to have any breeding stock left for the following year. There are two major methods for deciding which stock to keep. The first is to select one particular characteristic and concentrate all your attentions on it. With this method, the breeder will select rabbits that excel in this characteristic until he feels that the characteristic has become fixed within his stock. He then moves to concentrate on another characteristic until that too is fixed. Progress is slow but sure by this method. The rabbits culled are those that fail in the one point to be fixed.

The other method is to choose rabbits that show the most good points. The characteristics should be graded according to their im-

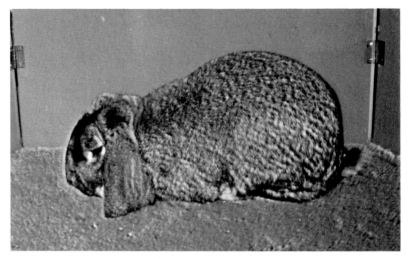

A solid colored French lop rabbit. The most common color of French lops is the agouti, or the color of wild rabbits.

A broken colored French lop rabbit. The body type must be massive and thickset. Note the simple and well-rounded dewlap.

A solid-colored English lop rabbit. The solid category includes selfs, shaded and agouti.

A broken colored English lop rabbit. Any of the colors together with white comprise the broken color category.

portance. Each rabbit can then be graded accordingly. Those that fall below the required standard should automatically be discarded. This method can be implemented by the breeder of meat rabbits with great success. He should grade the stock according to their litter size, growth rate, meat quality and pelt quality, although not necessarily in that order.

It should be obvious that more does than bucks are required for breeding. The selection of bucks should, therefore, be much more severe than for the does. The buck's qualities will differ from the doe's. The buck may be required to have a good fertility record. He will have to be able to sire a good number of above-average youngsters and will also be required to pass on his good qualities to his progeny.

Rabbit Breeds
And Judging Standards

The various breeds of rabbit are split into two main groups, the *fancy* types and the *fur* types. The fancy group includes the breeds that are kept for exhibition purposes. They are bred for their appearance, including body shape or type, size, color and pattern or coat markings. Both fur and fancy rabbit breeds are included in the group called *commercial* rabbits, which are raised for their meat.

FANCY RABBITS

The smallest fancy rabbit is the Netherland dwarf; the largest are the American, English and Flemish giants. Each breed of fancy rabbit has its own standard of excellence. The standard is the model of perfection around which every breeder tries to mold his stock. When fancy rabbits are judged at a show, they are compared to the ideal for their breed. The ideal specimen would receive 100 points out of a possible total of 100.

The total of 100 points is divided among the rabbit's head, type, color, coat, ears, eyes and other important characteristics. The highest number of points is assigned to the most important characteristic of that particular breed of rabbit. A rabbit may excel in one particular point but fail badly in other points.

The perfect specimen of any breed has never been produced. It is left entirely to the judge's discretion to decide how many points a rabbit will receive for any particular characteristic. The standard is a general guide, and the judge interprets it as he sees fit. For example, the standard for Polish or Britannia petite rabbit states that the rabbit be short, cobby and sprightly. The judge must decide exactly what is meant by these terms.

A new breed color of dwarf lop rabbit. Any color is acceptable provided that the fur appears good and lustrous. A French lop rabbit (below) with butterfly-shaped smut and marked areas on the head and neck.

A two-year-old English lop. Judges consider not only the length of the ears but also the substance or thickness. Paper-thin ears are faulted.

A chinchilla giganta rabbit. Breeders have found that very large breeds are not always profitable for the meat market. Their growth rate may be slow, and they will need much food. The meat-bone ratio may also be small.

FUR RABBITS

Rabbits in the fur group are also kept for exhibition purposes, but they are bred for their fur qualities rather than their body shape. The prime considerations when showing, rearing and judging fur rabbits are the texture and color of the animal's coat. Type plays a very small role in the general makeup of the fur rabbit. The ideal fur rabbit is an animal that provides a pelt that is excellent from the furrier's point of view. The coat must be uniform in color for the self-colored (self-colored means uniformly or solidly colored) rabbit. In the marked breeds, the markings and pattern must be clear and distinct.

A bad fault in the fur rabbit would be molting, which would make the coat uneven. Like the fancy rabbit, the fur rabbit is judged according to an ideal standard, but more points will be allotted to the coat of the fur rabbit than for any other characteristic.

Although rabbits are still used by furriers, they are not as much in demand as they were a few years ago, because imitation furs can now be made that do not possess the flaws that sometimes ruin animal pelts. In general, the fur rabbits are slightly larger than their fancy counterparts.

150

COMMERCIAL RABBITS

The commercial group of rabbits is not distinct from the fancy and fur breeds; instead it includes both of them. Commercial rabbits are kept and bred solely for their meat. Although the pelts from some of these rabbits are sold to furriers, the main objective is to obtain a fleshy carcass at an early age. Therefore, the larger breeds of rabbit are usually used, whether they are fur or fancy. The young rabbit should put on weight rapidly in order to be ready for market as soon as possible. Also, there should be very little waste when the carcass is dressed and ready for market.

SELECTING A BREED

Before purchasing stock, the newcomer to rabbits is advised to study the various breeds. There are many factors that should influence the final decision.

The novice is advised to start with only one breed. Often a beginner buys two or three different breeds. Each breed requires special attention, and an inexperienced breeder cannot cope with the problems involved. Because his attention is divided between two or three different breeds, the novice produces only mediocre herds. Sometimes the discouraged beginner will then abandon the hobby altogether. It is much better to select only one breed and to devote all your time and attention to one *good* herd.

The final choice of a breed depends on the careful consideration of many factors. Most important is to consider the use of the rabbit. If it is intended for exhibition, the novice can choose a fancy breed or a fur breed. The space allotted for the herd must be considered, and the fancier must decide whether he wants many small rabbits or a few big ones. There is also the question of financing the hobby: the cost of keeping the rabbits and of setting up a rabbitry.

The novice can incorporate the pleasure of showing his rabbits with a sideline as a rabbit meat producer. There would not be any real profit involved, as the ordinary backyard fancier could not hope to satisfy the demands of a customer who requires a large number of carcasses at regular intervals. The fancier could breed only enough stock to supply his own table and those of his relatives and a few friends.

In standing position a French lop shows the extent of its ears.

This red-eyed white Netherland dwarf mother rabbit is rather long in the body, but when mated with the right type of buck it produced typical Netherland dwarf bunnies. The Netherland dwarf breed has contributed to the formation of the dwarf lop.

The dwarf lop rabbit resembles a cuddly puppy and it is a very manageable pet. Agouti is the most common color in the dwarf lops.

By now the novice should have a clearer picture of the types of rabbit breeds. If a small fancy breed is desired, the Polish and Netherland dwarfs have much to offer. (The danger in keeping the small breeds is that the novice is likely to obtain as many of each color of that breed as possible. Once again the problem of divided attention creeps in, and the general standard of excellence is lowered.)

The medium-sized breeds include the Dutch, the English and the Silvers. The larger fancy rabbits are the French and English lops, the Belgian hare and the Giants.

THE ALASKA

This breed originated from Germany from Himalayan and argente rabbits. It is a medium-size breed; the registration weight of between six and a half to eight and a half pounds is required. There is no visible neck in this cobby or dumpy breed. The fur is intensely black and shiny on the surface, even the belly is black but it is matt and not as lustrous. The fur when parted should be at least one fourth of an inch colored black at the tips and the rest of dark slate blue. However, some isolated but evenly distributed white hairs are permissible. The eyes are dark brown and the toenails dark colored. Any lightness in these parts is considered a fault.

THE AMERICAN

The American is one of the many breeds of rabbits recognized by the American Rabbit Breeders Association. It comes in either blue or white coat. Their eyes should be pink in the white variety and blue in the blue variety. This is a medium size rabbit; ideal weight for bucks is 10 pounds and 11 pounds for does.

THE ANGORA

It is fitting that the Angora be listed among the first breeds because it begins with the first letter of the alphabet but also because it is one of the oldest breeds of rabbit and the forerunner of the fancy rabbit. The Angora is believed to have originated in Turkey hundreds of years ago. There is no definite proof of this, but it is worthwhile to note that other long-haired species of animal such as goats, sheep and cats are also said to have originated in Turkey.

The general appearance of the Angora should be as round as a ball. Many specimens, however, are too narrow-shouldered, making them look pear-shaped. This problem is sometimes caused by too much grooming. The English Angora is adorned with what are called "furnishings." These are growths of wool on the extreme tips of the ears and front feet. The ears should be well covered with a ball-like tuft of wool, but they should also have a fur covering all over the outside of the ear from the base of the ear right up to the tufts. The front feet are similarly adorned and have foot pads of wool, which unfortunately cannot be seen when the Angora sits in a crouched position. The eye color is rich ruby red.

Since the introduction of the usual white or albino Angora, some very beautiful colored Angoras have been bred. The most popular of these is the smoke, but there are also blue, black and chinchillated varieties.

Another breed of Angora which is not often seen is the French Angora. This breed is slightly larger than the English; it is heavier in bone and weighs eight pounds and over. The ears and forefeet lack the furnishings of its English cousin.

THE ARGENTE DE CHAMPAGNE

The Argente de Champagne was bred and kept in France for many years. It was used both as a fur and meat-bearing animal by the French peasants who raised it. The name Champagne is misleading, because it does not refer to the color of the rabbit, but is an indication that it comes from the Champagne district of France. The breed itself is actually a silvered color. The French word *argente* means silver. In England the argente de Champagne is a fur breed, but in France it is a fancy breed.

The actual color is threefold. The undercolor is a dark slate blue, and the top color is whitish blue shot through with long black hairs. Evenness of color is very important in this breed, because an imbalance detracts from the coat's unusual appeal.

The black hairs in the coat must be evenly spread to create the right effect. If there are too many black hairs, the coat appears too dark; if there are too few, the coat looks washy. In general, the color including that on the head, ears and legs should be even.

Note the thick and rough-looking coat of this red-eyed white Netherland dwarf rabbit bred in Germany. It is also called ermine. According to the standards a white Netherland dwarf rabbit (below) must be pure white; a yellowish tinge is faulted. They can have either red or blue eyes only.

A red-eyed Netherland dwarf rabbit. Netherland dwarfs are bred as selfs, shaded, agouti, tan, patterned and any other varieties.

A blue-eyed Netherland dwarf rabbit.

In earlier specimens of the breed, those with darker heads usually had a darker undercolor and those with light heads had a light undercolor.

The young, on being weaned, are self-black in color; the silvered effect takes place gradually. The argente de Champagne is a slightly larger than medium-sized breed, weighing in the region of eight pounds.

The general type is of moderate proportions, the ears carried erect and rounded at the tips.

THE ARGENTE BLEU

Although of the same color pattern as the Champagne, the argente bleu has a completely different body type. It is a much more compact rabbit, having a cobby appearance and short neck. The cobbiness is due to the broad loins and well-developed hind-quarters coupled with short, fine-boned front legs. The total weight is about six pounds.

The color, too, is different from that of the Champagne. There is an undercolor of lavender and a top coat of bluish white. The long black hairs of the Champagne are replaced by long blue hairs. This gives the whole rabbit a bluish cast that is very attractive when viewed from a distance. Another difference from the Champagne is that the coat should lie flat and smooth and not open as in the former.

The blue has been successfully mated with the Champagne, but there is a tendency to alter each color by this method of breeding. Because of the difference in weight in the two colors, difficulties are often encountered.

A dewlap (fold or folds of skin hanging from the throat) in either the buck or doe is a serious fault.

THE ARGENTE BRUN

This breed is exactly the same as the blue except the color is brown.

It is not a well-known color and is rarely seen now. It was brought into England about 1920 from France. Its unpopularity made it very rare indeed. In 1941 it was recreated by H.D. Dowie. Dowie did this by crossing cremes with blues, which produced silvered agoutis. The agoutis were mated to Havanas and produced silvered blacks. When these were mated amongst

158

themselves, they produced the argente brun. Brown Beverens have since been used to improve the coat qualities of the contemporary brun.

THE ARGENTE CREME

The creme is the smallest of the argente breed. The color of this rabbit is exquisite. No other color of fur or fancy rabbit can compare to it. The undercolor is bright orange and the top color creamy white interspersed with long orange hairs.

Although it is much smaller, the type is similar to the Champagne. As in the argente brun, the coat should lie flat and sleek, adding to the beauty of the whole pelt. Condition is very important in the creme. Without good condition, the coat loses its appeal and unusual look.

THE AMERICAN CHECKERED GIANT

Although it is called the American giant, this breed originated in Germany. Its origins are a mystery. Some authorities maintain that it was bred from the Flemish giant and a wild white hare. According to this theory, the offspring were mated together and inbred to keep the black and white markings. Other experts say that checkered lops first appeared and were bred with the Flemish in order to reduce the size of the ears. In appearance, the American is very much like the English spot but lacks the chain of spots of the latter and is much larger. The first checkered giants seen in America about 1910 were much smaller than those of today. Today the ideal weight for buck is 11 pounds or over and 12 pounds or over for does.

The checkered giant has a very distinctive body type. It is long and well-arched with medium-broad hindquarters and body carried well off the ground. A bad fault is the lack of proper back arch, short, coupled or cut-off hindquarters.

Two colors are recognized, black and blue. All colored markings—butterfly or nose markings, eye circles, cheek spots, ears, spine markings, tail and side markings—are to be clear and distinct.

THE BELGIAN HARE

The Belgian hare at one time was the most popular fancy rabbit. It was responsible for bringing the domestic rabbit to the attention of thousands of people both in the United Kingdom and the United States.

Baby Netherland dwarf rabbits, all under five months. Several varieties (red-eyed white, Siamese smoke, orange, Himalayan and chinchilla) are recognizable.

A sealpoint Netherland dwarf rabbit.

Although called a hare, it is in fact a rabbit. It was once believed that the Belgian could be successfully crossed with a true wild hare, but this is not true.

The Belgian originated in Flanders and there is evidence to indicate it was bred down from a now-extinct breed known as the Patagonian. The Patagonian, incidentally, was the forerunner of the Flemish giant. The early Belgians were nothing like they are today. They were much more heavily built and much less graceful.

The Belgian was imported to England where it was selectively bred until the present-day form was produced. The Belgian generated much interest; during its boom period, the Belgian was bred for both its exhibition properties and its meat-producing qualities.

The genetic color of the Belgian is agouti, but the deep chestnut hue of the fur was produced by crossing the Belgian with brown Beverens. The deep chestnut color is very attractive. It is bordered by black ticking along the entire length of the body and also around the ears. A common failing is the appearance of gray hairs along the flanks. If the Belgian hare is not fit, it does not look as it should. Fitness is very important. The coat must shine as though it were polished mahogany, the flesh must be firm and the eyes bright and gleaming. A Belgian in such condition is a work of art. It requires much practice and perseverance.

The typical Belgian pose must, of course, be quite natural. If the animal is flat-footed, it does not look right; if it has to be held in the posed position, it lacks style. The pose should be graceful with an arched back and fine delicate bone. The ears should be about five inches long and slope backwards slightly. The Belgian's eyes are a very attractive deep hazel color that blend with the coat's color. They should be bold and bright with a general look of alertness.

The Belgian hare is a very distinctive rabbit and often takes top honors at rabbit shows.

THE BEVEREN

The Beveren is one of the oldest and largest of the fur rabbits. It was first bred in Beveren, a small town near Antwerp in Belgium. About 1915, during World War I, the Beveren became very popular in England because meat was very scarce. The flesh of the Beveren was more important than the fur at the time. The first Beverens were blue; later blacks, browns and whites were produced. The color must be deep and solid. The presence of white hairs in coloreds and silvering are common faults that must be avoided if the rabbit is to produce good colored youngster. Silvering was a common fault in the early blues. Because it was initially believed that they were too dark, the blues were crossed with light colored rabbits of other breeds and the silvering became prevalent.

The texture of the coat is intensely dense and thick. The fur should feel exquisitely silky and soft. Any harshness or woolliness is a fault. The desired length of fur is about one inch to one and a half inches. An interesting feature of the white Beveren is its clear blue eyes, distinguishing it from many of the other white fur breeds. The Beveren is the largest of the fur breeds, weighing seven to 10 pounds. The body is long but broad, with a distinct mandolin shape. The head is broad with a distinct curve from the forehead to the tip of the nose. The ears are long and broad with good substance or thickness, held in a "V" shape. The ear color should match that of the body perfectly. The ears of some Beverens tend to be a shade darker, throwing off the color balance.

The blue Beveren should be a lavender shade right down to the skin; the white should be pure white with no hint of yellow stain or colored hairs; the black should be deep, jet black with a dark blue undercolor and the brown should be an even shade of nutria brown with a beige undercolor.

THE BLANC DE BOUSCAT

As its name suggests, the Bouscat is of French origin. It was produced by Mssr. Paul Dulon of Gironde in 1910. The Bouscat is very popular on the European continent both as an exhibition fur rabbit and as a meat rabbit.

The Bouscat is believed to have been produced from the Angora, argente Champagne and albino Flemish giant. With this ancestry, it should be evident that the Bouscat is a fairly large rabbit, weighing about 12 pounds for the buck and up to 14 pounds for the doe. White is the only color and the fur is like the Beveren, dense and silky.

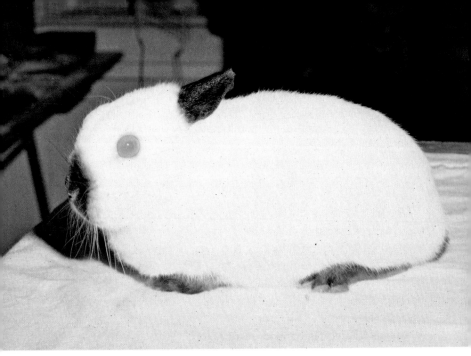

A Himalayan Netherland dwarf rabbit.

A Siamese sable Netherland dwarf rabbit.

A smoke colored Netherland dwarf rabbit.

An agouti Netherland dwarf rabbit.

The head is strong and broad, very rounded and well-set on the shoulders. Although it is a large rabbit, the fineness of bone is impressive like all meat-producing rabbits. The body is long and the back has a slight curve, starting behind the head and ending just in front of the haunches. The ears are long, well-rounded at the tips and held in a V-shaped position similar to the Beveren.

The blanc de Bouscat, almost unknown in the United States, is also quite rare in England, although it does enjoy a small group of followers.

THE BLANC DE HOTOT

The blanc de Hotot also originated in France, but it is much less well known than the Bouscat. In general, the texture and quality of the fur are very similar to the Bouscat with the exception that the Hotot has black eyelashes and a very fine black line around the eyes in the form of spectacles. Little is known of how the breed was produced, but it is almost certainly an old breed that was used for its meat qualities.

The type of the Hotot is much more thickset than the Bouscat, giving the rabbit a squarish look. It is also a little smaller, measuring between eight and 10 inches in length.

THE BRITISH GIANT

According to the standards of the British Rabbit Council the British giant rabbit is a large breed weighing not less than 12½ pounds for does and 11½ pounds for bucks. An entrant that weighs more than 15 pounds gets extra points, while another one weighing less than the minimum weight requirements is penalized.

This rabbit has a large, long and flat body. The front and hind quarters are also broad. The head must likewise be broad (narrow heads are faulted) and the ears must be erect. Size must not be on account of excessive fat or bagginess.

The coat is judged for its density and thickness (three-quarters to an inch long). The accepted colors are white (true white, not cream, with blue or pink eyes), black (black to blue, with blue or brown eyes), dark steel gray (evenly ticked, with brown eyes), brown gray (evenly ticked, with blue, gray or brown eyes) and blue (with blue gray or brown eyes).

THE CALIFORNIAN

The Californian is one of the more contemporary breeds of rabbit. It was produced in the United States in 1923. The creation of this breed was not an accident. It was painstakingly raised by George West, who wanted a better commercial rabbit than those available at the time. He began by crossing a Himalayan with a chinchilla. The progeny from this mating were mated to New Zealand whites. The end product was a large, meaty, well-proportioned rabbit with Himalayan markings. It took quite some time before the Californian was recognized. In 1939 the breed was officially registered by the American Rabbit Breeders Association. It is now reared the world over as a good meat-producing animal on par with any other commercial rabbit.

The entire body color is pure white with the black point markings of the Himalayan although the nose blaze is not as pronounced. The body is medium long, the back slightly rounded but full on the sides and shoulders.

THE CHINCHILLA

The chinchilla was one of the very first really important fur breeds. Like many other fur breeds, it came from France.

The French rabbit breeder Mssr. M.J. Dybowski is credited with producing this beautiful rabbit. The actual production claims of this man have always been in some doubt. One theory is that the chin, as it is more often called, came from Serbia and that Mssr. Dybowski merely improved on it and popularized the breed.

However, the popular theory is that Mssr. Dybowski crossed a wild rabbit with a blue Beveren and a Himalayan. The litters from the Himalayan doe and the Beveren doe were interbred and by a process of selection the early chin was produced. These early chins were very heavy-boned, similar to the giant breeds. The color of these rabbits was generally very poor. A black tan was used to try to improve the ticking and as a result other breeds were produced including the Siamese and marten sables.

In April, 1913, the chinchilla was exhibited for the first time and later that year it was given the "prize of honor" at the big show in Paris. When the first chinchillas came to England, they caused quite a sensation. A silver cup was offered for the best chin at an

A pair of Netherland dwarf rabbits of contrasting self colors. Many varieties of this breed are recognized (selfs, shaded, patterned, etc.).

A New Zealand white rabbit bred in England. White fur is preferred commercially because it can be dyed to other colors and patterns to simulate more expensive pelts.

A New Zealand white rabbit. This rabbit breed is the most widely bred rabbit for the table, the fur industry and the laboratory.

English show. The price for good quality furs went sky high. The chin appeared in America in 1919, where it caused just as much of a sensation.

The main attribute of this popular breed is, of course, the color and pattern of the pelt, which closely resembles that of the much-prized pelt of the true wild chinchilla. The undercolor of the fur should be slate blue at the base, the middle portion pearl gray merging into white and tipped with black. It should be noted that the slate blue base should be wider than the pearl portion. The whole of the pelt should be ticked with long black guard hairs that may be wavy or even.

Generally the flanks and chest are slightly lighter colored than the back; the neck is just a shade lighter than the chest and flanks. The triangle at the nape of the neck is light pearl gray as are the eye circles. The ears are laced with black. The belly and underside of the tail are white with a slate blue undercolor.

There are many arguments as to the correct chinchilla color. Some are obviously much too dark and some much too light. These arguments, along with those regarding pearling, are very complicated.

The texture of the fur is of prime importance. Without good texture, the color and pearling will be of inferior quality. The fur should be soft and dense; by no means should it be flyback nor should it be too long.

The Angora has been used successfully in the make up of the chinchilla, giving the coat its full density. It has also produced some bad faults, the most common of which is the appearance of woolly coats. Light-colored cheeks are also a direct result of the Angora introduction, as is a too large white area at the nape of the neck. Having barred feet is faulted.

Although adult chinchilla rabbits can weigh 5½ to 6¾ lbs., the standard calls for fine bone. In this respect, many rabbits fail.

THE AMERICAN CHINCHILLA

There are two types of American chinchilla, the standard type, which is very much like the English version, and the American chinchilla, which is slightly larger. The American was at one time called the heavyweight chinchilla and is a result of selecting the largest of the standard chins and aiming for a larger, more meaty, type of rabbit. The length is medium, but the hips are rounded and full. The back of the American chin has a slight and gradual arch starting at the nape of the neck and finishing at the rump.

THE CHINCHILLA GIGANTA

The chinchilla giganta was produced in England by Chris Wren in the early 1920's. It was reared for the sole purpose of combining better meat production with the attribute of the attractive chinchilla coat.

As a meat rabbit, the giganta is almost perfect; it quickly reaches the required growth rate. The pelt has caused some controversy within the rabbit world. Some say that it is equal in quality to the normal chinchilla, while others maintain that it is much too dark for high-class pelt work. The giganta's coat is certainly a little harsher and darker, but some really large pelts can be obtained from good-sized specimens. A maximum weight limit of 12 lbs. is placed on the giganta.

The giganta has two additional differences from the normal chinchilla. Firstly, barred feet are not a fault in the giganta. Secondly, unlike most fur breeds, the giganta carries its ears slightly sloped backward and open at the top, forming a distinct V when viewed from the front.

THE AMERICAN GIANT CHINCHILLA

The American giant chinchilla is another type of American chinchilla. It was derived by crossing the standard chin with Flemish giants. Ed Stahl of Missouri is the original producer of this breed, which is important for its meat qualities.

The basic type is much the same as the American chin, but the giant is much fuller with a good meaty saddle. Adult bucks weigh about 13 to 14 pounds and the does about 14 to 15 pounds.

THE DUTCH

Everybody knows the Dutch rabbit when they see it. The distinctive markings set it apart from all other breeds of rabbit. The Dutch is perhaps the most popular fancy rabbit in the world. It is reputed to have originated in Holland and was one of the earliest fancy breeds to reach the English shores.

A smoke pearl
Netherland
dwarf rabbit.

An agouti
Netherland
dwarf rabbit.

This is the
result of a cross
between a
marten and a
white ermine
Netherland
dwarf rabbit.

A Netherland dwarf rabbit of mixed origin. Note the white spots on the nose and forehead. A marten sable Netherland dwarf rabbit. (below)

Both the English and American standards are very precise and only those specimens close to the ideal ever win any major honors.

The Dutch pattern or markings are the result of a genetic factor and they appear in other forms of small livestock such as rats, mice, cavies, etc. The faults in the pattern are numerous. Perhaps this is why the perfect Dutch rabbit has yet to be bred. The Dutch rabbit is bred in black, which is by far the most popular color, and also in blue, steel gray, tortoiseshell, yellow and chocolate.

The Dutch rabbit's head shows the faults perhaps more than any other part of the body because the fur is shorter and the markings more clear-cut.

The blaze is the strip of white flanked on either side by the cheeks of the predominant color of the rabbit. If the cheeks are too wide, it gives the impression that the blaze is too narrow. If the cheeks are too narrow, the blaze is too wide. The cheeks actually begin between the ears, go just over the eye and down the sides of the face to just below the jaws.

A common fault on the cheeks is that they "pull on the smellers." This is Dutch rabbit jargon to indicate that the line of the cheeks touches the whiskers. As the line continues, it should just border the actual cheek bones, but viewed from the side, no white should be visible below the cheek line. Dutch rabbits that carry these faults also have "full necks." A full neck means that the colored part between the ears continues over the head and onto the nape of the neck.

The ears play a very important role in the composition of the head. They should not be too long but should be in proportion to the size of the rabbit. The ears should be well-covered with fur and held erect, solid in color with no foreign marks such as white patches.

The saddle is the colored part of the Dutch markings, which should total almost two thirds of the body. It extends from a few inches behind the shoulders and encompasses all the rest of the body. The line of the saddle should just touch the shoulders and continue right around the body in a straight line. Under the belly, the line is termed the undercut. This is where the more common faults are to be found. Often the undercut is ragged and uneven; in some cases it even runs out altogether. The saddle falls prey to these same faults, but they are rarely seen on the showbench because such a specimen would be disregarded by the breeders. In poorly marked Dutch rabbits the saddle runs to a point between the shoulders and is sometimes skewed to one side.

The stops are the markings of white on the hind feet which look like socks. They carry the same faults as the saddle and undercut, out under and ragged demarcation lines. Frequently if one stop is out, the other will follow suit.

The ideal length of the stops is one and one-quarter inches; they are often either too short or too long.

Although the color is the last consideration in examining a Dutch, it is just as important as the other features. A good black Dutch rabbit should be jet black in color. Frequently a rusty tinge creeps in to mar this color. In adults it may be that the rabbit is about to molt, but in young Dutch it is often caused by breeding. The mixing of colors, especially black to steel gray, is usually the cause of this fault.

Blue Dutch are apt to be light colored at their extremities, but rustiness is much less common in this color.

Blacks and blues can be bred together because blue is dilute black. However, there is a tendency for the blue shade to become too dark if this practice is overused. A medium shade of blue should always be the objective.

Steel gray is perhaps the second most popular Dutch. The color usually lasts for years without fading. The actual shade is dark gray interspersed with steel ticking. The main fault with the steel color is that the ticking is not as pronounced as it could be.

Brown gray, which can be either light or dark brown, is another shade of gray. The color is basically the same as steel, except the ground color is brown. A common fault with this color is that the undercut may be barely discernible and the cheeks are sometimes too light in color.

Chocolate Dutch are becoming more and more popular. The actual color is deep dark brown; frequently like the blues, they tend to be light at the extremities.

The tortoiseshell Dutch is a yellow ground with shadings of black on the haunches, ears and cheeks. The main fault is that the shadings often become smudgy and spoil the appearance of the rabbit.

The yellow Dutch is somewhat of a backward relation of the tor-

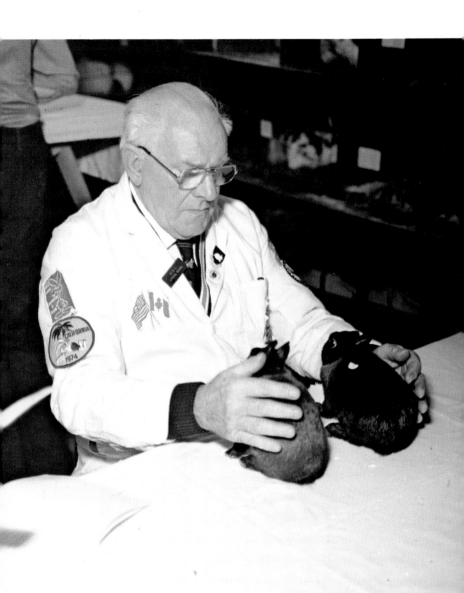

A pair of Netherland dwarf rabbits being evaluated by Mr. Peter Cage of England. This is his favorite breed.

A Netherland dwarf rabbit with imperfect Dutch pattern. The separation between the colors must be clean or unbroken and not ragged as in this specimen.

This photo shows why Netherland dwarf rabbits are very popular as house pets; they do not require much room.

toiseshell. Yellows are also frequently light colored on the extremities and also tend to show some tortoiseshell shadings. The yellow's markings are usually not as eye-catching as the other colors, but occasionally a really outstanding yellow turns up and steals the major honors at a top show.

In all colors, the general type of the Dutch is the same: it should be neither too large nor too small. If it is too large, the whole idea of type is lost; if it is too small, it appears racy. Cobbiness should be the main consideration. One advantage in the breeding of Dutch rabbits is that the newborn litter can be inspected very early and those that are mismarked can be detected at a glance and removed to afford the better-marked babies more chance of survival. Often experienced Dutch fanciers mate two does at the same time. After removing the unwanted young from both litters, they foster the remainder of one litter with the other doe. Thus more litters can be reared and the chances of breeding a good rabbit are improved. Young Dutch can be exhibited as soon as they are able to look after themselves, but the general practice is to wait until they are strong enough to withstand the rigors of exhibition. Dutch rabbits are not the easiest breed to rear successfully, but when a good one does come along it is well worth all the trouble, hard work and heartbreaks.

THE TRI-COLORED DUTCH

This rabbit is not to be confused with the tortoiseshell Dutch mentioned previously. The color which makes up the pattern is similar to the harlequin, complete with stripes. The pattern of the Dutch is also incorporated into this, which makes the rabbit very attractive. The ears are colored according to the harlequin pattern, which is one black ear and one yellow or golden orange ear. The face is divided into half of each color, but the blaze of the Dutch must be present and should be as wide as possible.

The front legs and feet are completely white, as in the Dutch. The Dutch saddle is also present, but into this is incorporated the alternate bands of black and golden orange of the harlequin. The hind feet stops of the Dutch complete the pattern with each one being a different color, one black leg and one golden orange leg. Little is known about the origin of the tri-color Dutch, but it is almost certainly of Dutch or French breeding.

This rabbit has never been very popular because of the complication of the pattern. It is bred and shown on the European continent and appears occasionally at some of the larger shows in England

THE ENGLISH

The English, like the Dutch, is very popular. It is also one of the oldest fancy breeds, In 1849 a description was published of a rabbit that would seem to be an early English. The description was contained in *A complete directory for the proper treatment, breeding, feeding and management of all kinds of domestic poultry, pigeons, rabbits, etc.* The most interesting feature of this description referred to the "butterfly smut and chain spots," although the breed was not actually termed the English at the time. As its name implies the English is purely an English breed. For some time the English was kept by the majority of British fanciers because of its novelty. After a boom from 1855 to 1860, nothing was heard of the breed until about 1880.

At that time only the black color was known; a few years later tortoiseshells appeared followed by blues, grays and chocolates. Today all these colors are seen at almost every big show.

The English is basically a white rabbit with black markings. The black ears are held erect, about four inches in length. Any white hairs or patches are a fault. The eyes are encircled with black, giving the rabbit a spectacled look. A common fault in the eye circle is that it is too heavy and ragged in appearance. To complete the head markings, there is a butterfly smut covering the whole nose. This should be solid black in color and shaped to resemble the outline of a butterfly. Any white markings here are a fault. Just below the eye, on either side of the face, there should be a small black spot. Unfortunately this spot often runs into the eye circle or is so lightly marked as to be almost unnoticeable.

The entire length of the spine is marked with a herring-bone pattern. The saddle, as this line is called, should run from the base of the ears, along the full length of the rabbit and onto the top side of the tail. Faults here include blotchy marking, thin and undefined herring-bone, broken saddle, and a mixture of white hairs contained within the saddle color.

A young New Zealand white rabbit. The New Zealand white is the number one commercial breed because of its fast growth rate and white fur. It is now bred in many countries.

A New Zealand

An adult New Zealand white rabbit.

An English spot rabbit. The eye circles must not touch any other spot on the cheek.

The most elusive characteristic of the English rabbit is the chain of spots running along each side of the flanks. The chain begins in small spots at either side of the neck and runs in a curve down to the sides of the belly where the spots gradually increase in size and continue over the haunches. The greatest number of faults occur in the spots forming the chain; too heavy is as bad as too light, too many is as bad as too few, often the chain is completely broken. Although each limb should also carry a distinct spot, those on the front limbs are more highly prized. The sweep of the chain gives the English a very graceful look. But if the type is bad, the pleasing qualities of the markings are lost. The belly of the English rabbit has teat spots. These should consist of six clear and distinct spots.

The rabbit should almost lie on the table, just keeping the belly clear of the surface, the back arched and the loins well rounded.

The English is one of the more difficult breeds to rear to perfection. In an average litter there are about 50 percent marked young, 25 percent self blacks and 25 percent charlies. The charlie English is really an incompletely marked rabbit. Instead of a full butterfly smut, there is only a small moustache, the ears are colored but the rest of the markings are either completely missing or so light as to be indiscernible.

The genetics of the English rabbit is fascinating as it is heterozygous. Thus it cannot breed true to type. When breeding the English, if the well-marked rabbit is mated to a charlie the chances of producing well-marked youngsters increases. In some cases 100 percent success has been achieved. If charlies are mated together, only charlies are produced. Two self English will only produce selfs if mated together.

The attractive pattern of the English rabbit's coat has been used for fur craft. Usually the product is only a novelty, but the quality of the fur is excellent. Because of its size, the English can also be used for meat production. The meat has a low offal content and the young English grows very fast and makes a presentable carcass for frying purposes. In the United States this breed is known as the English Spot.

THE FLEMISH GIANT

The Flemish giant is the largest rabbit exhibited in England. The Flemish originated in the area of Flanders and is included in the list of early fancy rabbits. The Flemish was known by the name Patagonian for many years. The early Flemish were prized for their great size; as the standard was revised, color took first preference in the allocation of points. The weight is of secondary importance to size. The larger the better, no matter how much the rabbit weighs.

The main feature of the Flemish type is squareness and good width of body. Without this feature, the Flemish looks racy and does not display the huge proportions of good type. The forefront should be large and square, the hindquartes rounded and full. Between the head and rump, the body should be perfectly flat but yet large and wide. Does are allowed to carry a large dewlap, but it must be rounded and evenly spread.

Color is of the utmost importance. The first color was steel gray. The gray must be very dark over the entire rabbit's body. A darker face is allowed. Rustiness is a common failing with this color, perhaps due to the mixing of the colors, especially with sandy colored rabbits. The belly and underside of the Flemish is white with a dark undercolor. The legs should be strong in bone and carried firmly. Any tendency to light bone lends a baggy appearance to the Flemish.

A New Zealand black rabbit.

A New Zealand red rabbit.

A lynx palomino rabbit. The palomino is exclusively American in origin. It is a fur and meat breed.

A golden palomino rabbit.

The head is full and bold, with the ears carried erect.

The Flemish makes a very good meat rabbit; during the war years, it was kept in many backyards for this purpose.

THE FLORIDA WHITE

The Florida white is another breed that was created by fanciers with a specific need in mind. The breed originated in Florida to satisfy the demand for a medium-sized rabbit with good meat qualities that could also be used in research stations. The Dutch and Polish were used in the initial cross and the New Zealand white was added at a later stage.

The type is a rather cobby, compact rabbit, the hips and hindquarters well rounded, gently sloping down to well-proportioned shoulders. The head is small and the ears short, well-rounded at the tips, well-set on the head. The fur is pure white, short and dense, with roll-back properties.

The ideal weight for bucks and does is five pounds and the registration weight for both sexes is between four and six pounds.

THE HAVANA

The Havana is a very well-known fur breed of European origin. Although its ancestry is uncertain, it is known that the first Havana appeared in a litter bred from a Dutch doe that was stabled with other breeds. The sire of the Havana was never established. Bred in a stable near Utrecht, Holland, the Havana was first exhibited at Utrecht in 1899.

Known at that time as the beaver, it was known under that name in France several years later. The popularity of the breed spread quickly; it was shown in Switzerland in 1905 and in Germany in 1907. One year later it was imported into England by a Miss Illingworth who exhibited the first Havana at a show in Cambridge in 1909. The Havana rapidly became popular all over England. In 1920 the National Havana Club was formed. In 1916, the Havana was introduced into the United States, where the blue Havana was produced by Owen Stamm several years later. The Havana is exclusively a fur breed. Its deep, rich, chocolate brown pelt has been compared to the Havana cigar. As the Florida white, the Havana type is inclined to be short and cobby. The head is small, the neck very short. The rump and hindquarters are rounded and full, sloping to well-developed shoulders. The bone is fine; very few specimens have the fineness of bone of the ideal Havana.

One of the most attractive features of the Havana is the rich, ruby-eyed glow of the eye. Although the eyes should be the same color as the body, they glow ruby red in a darkened room.

The main faults concerning type are that many rabbits appear too long in barrel and flat along the spine. This type of Havana should be avoided because type is allotted almost as many points as the coat. Compact does not indicate a very short rabbit, but rather one that is well-proportioned and well-balanced.

An important feature of the type is the shape of the head and ears. The head is relatively short and broad, especially in the buck. Pinched noses and long ears are often related to long bodies. A rabbit that has one of these faults has bad type. The ears should be held erect, broad at the base, tapering gently to pointed tips and carried closely together.

The rich color of the Havana should be even all over the body with no light patches or odd white hairs. Ginger patches were a common failing in the early Havanas, but these patches are now more rare. Yet the Havana should never be shown while it is molting as the different colored parts of the rabbit are evident. New, darker fur contrasts with the old, lighter fur. Although the color and coat quality are closely coupled, the coat is slightly more important. Without good coat quality, the color cannot look its best.

The ideal coat is one inch long, very dense and glossy, fine in texture and lying close to the body. Strangely, thin-coated Havanas excel in color. But because color is of secondary importance, these specimens should probably be disregarded in favor of the better coated rabbits. Although the fur is soft, it should lie very close to the body, which makes it extremely attractive. Any woolliness renders the coat open and staring, losing the deep, glossy sheen that adds the final finish to the perfect Havana.

THE HARLEQUIN

This breed of fancy rabbit is the mystery of the rabbit world. The harlequin is bred in black, the most popular color, and in blue, brown and lilac, as well as three different coat types: normal coated, rex and astrex. The latter is very rarely seen.

A black Polish rabbit. The American type of Polish rabbit is small and round-bodied, like a Netherland dwarf rabbit.

A chocolate Polish rabbit.

A blue-eyed white Polish rabbit.

A ruby-eyed Polish rabbit. The American Polish is exhibited with the belly close to the floor.

A smoke pearl Britannia petite. The English Polish rabbit is classed separately in the United States as the Britannia petite to distinguish it from the American Polish rabbit.

In addition to the orange-patterned harlequin there is the magpie harlequin. Identical to the normal harlequin in pattern, the orange is replaced by white in the magpie.

Originally produced in France, the harlequin was a very popular breed in Normandy and the Montmartre suburbs of Paris. Like the Dutch, the harlequin is of Barbancon ancestry. The first harlequin appeared at a show in Paris in 1887, but it was not until 1891 that the breed was described in the journal *L'Aviculteur.*

Describing the harlequin is very complicated, as the pattern is one of alternating contrasts. The ears are opposite colors. In the black harlequin, one ear is black and the other orange. The head is also divided and the colors are reversed. On the side of the orange ear, the face is black; on the side of the black ear, the face is orange. The dividing line between the face colors should start well between the ears and progress in a straight line down the face and under the chin. In some specimens, the chest is also divided in the same way, but it is not required in the standard and should be disregarded. The whole body is alternately striped with orange and black from just behind the shoulders to the rump. These rings of alternating color need not be complete and encircle the body, as long as they are complete around the back. The harlequin's feet also alternate in color: the forefeet should be black on the orange side of the face and orange on the black side of the face. Thus, the hind feet are also opposite the forefeet. A truly checkered rabbit if there ever was one!

Blacks should be deep, lustrous black with no hint of rust or shading. The orange, described in the standard as golden orange, should be as bright as possible. Occasionally white feet appear; they should be regarded as a fault rather than a disqualification.

Although the type of the harlequin is representative of the meat and fur rabbit, it is classified as a fancy rabbit. The head is long and broad between the eyes. The ears should be four to five inches long, carried erect and slightly open at the tops. The body is muscular, well-developed and mandolin-shaped—resembling the shape of an upside-down mandolin.

The flesh should be firm and not soft, a feature that made the harlequin popular as a meat rabbit during the war years. The limbs are of medium bone, strong and well-muscled. The general eye color is hazel, but brown or blue eyes are also seen occasionally.

The appearance of brindling spoils the markings of many harlequins. Brindling is a result of the chinchillating factor in the genetic make-up of the harlequin. The coat is fine in texture, very soft and dense, about an inch in length.

THE HARLEQUIN REX

The pattern of the harlequin rex is the same as for the normal harlequin, but the fur is characteristic of the best rex-coated rabbits. The texture is fine and very silky, intensely dense and level. It is difficult to breed a good-patterned, rex-coated harlequin, but really good specimens are held in high esteem. The rex type has a graceful look, with a gentle slope up to well-rounded hindquarters. The head is short and broad unlike that of the normal harlequin which is elongated. Dewlaps are allowed in the rex harlequin, but they should be well-rounded and not excessive. There is no mention of a dewlap in the normal-coated harlequin standard.

The harlequin astrex is of the same type as the rex with the exception that the fur is slightly shorter and curly over the whole of the body. The feet, ears and tail are normal coated.

The harlequin-patterned Dutch is treated separately as tri-colored Dutch and is discussed elsewhere.

THE HIMALAYAN

The Himalayan has been known by a number of other names. In eastern Europe it was called the "Russian" and later was known as the "Egyptian Smut." The Himalayan's origin is rather obscure; it probably originated in China, where there were once thousands of this breed.

The Himalayan first came to the West as a zoological oddity known as "the black-nosed rabbit from China." It is truly an international breed that can now be found in almost every country in the world.

The Himalayan is a white rabbit with colored extremities: the ears, nose, feet and tail are colored. The colors recognized in the standards are black, chocolate, blue and lilac.

The Himalayan gene is dominant to true albino, but it is recessive to all other genes. The young are born with a grayish

A smoke pearl Britannia petite.

A white Britannia petite.

A marten sable Polish rabbit.

cast all over the body that gradually decreases until they are pure white. The appearance of colored extremities occurs at the age of three to four weeks. The color is initially very pale; as the rabbit molts it becomes more definable.

Extremes of temperature have a drastic effect on the amount of color present on the young Himalayan. The colder the air temperature, the more color. In really cold conditions, many youngsters develop body and eye stains—patches of color appearing around the eyes and any part of the rabbit's body. These stains are considered a fault when the rabbit is judged at a show.

The Himalayan type is one of sleek gracefulness, sometimes described as snaky. The head is long and pointed, the ears held erect and pointed at the tips, the body is long and slender with fine bone. The hindfeet are also fine in bone and carried well tucked under the haunches.

The markings are more important than type in judging the Himalayan. The nose smut should be carried well up the face to a point between the eyes. A good sound color without a brownish tinge, putty nose or any other white hairs is essential. The leg markings are known as stockings and should be carried well up to the elbow joint on the forefeet and beyond this on the hind feet. A common failing is that the limbs are usually less well-colored than any other colored part of the Himalayan.

The ears should be as short as possible, but well-colored without any presence of rusty shade or white hairs. Good-colored ears are usually well-covered with fur; bad-colored ears seem to have a bare edge along the entire length of the ear. The Himalayan's tail is carried well tucked in; it should be colored underneath as well as on top. The Himalayan's eye is a sparkling pink color. Any paleness in the eye detracts from the bright appearance and makes the rabbit look sullen. The pelt should be smooth in texture, short and as pure white as possible without any yellow tinge or cast.

Docile by nature, the Himalayan makes an ideal rabbit for the novice. It can even be kept as a child's pet without fear of the animal biting its young handler.

THE LILAC

The lilac is believed by many authorities to have originated as a sport in a litter of Havanas. Others say that it was bred by crossing a blue Beveren with a Havana. The second method, first accomplished by Professor R.C. Punnet in 1922, has been described in detail. The litter from this cross, which was all black, carried the factor for dilution and, when bred among themselves, produced blue, black, brown, and lilac. The lilac is a dilute brown.

The lilac was originally known as the Cambridge blue. The Gouda, a lilac-colored Dutch rabbit, was produced two years earlier than the English lilac. The lilac bears an unmistakable resemblance to its Havana forebears in type. The body is short and cobby with well-developed hind quarters. The head is short; the short ears are held upright.

Many of the earlier lilacs were much heavier boned with thinner, harsher coats that were inclined to be flyback. Another common failing with the early lilacs was the abundance of white hairs under the armpits. It is very rare indeed to find a lilac today with these faults. Contemporary coats are much denser, giving the lilac a pelt of exceptional softness.

Color, too, has improved considerably. The pinkish dove shade is much more uniform over the entire rabbit; the blue cast is much less common. A good lilac is pleasing to the eye; the coat should be deep and soft to the touch. There should also be a warm glow to the rabbit resulting from the pinkish dove shade of the fur, which should have a lustrous look.

THE LOP

"King of the Fancy" is a phrase used exclusively to describe the lop for two reasons. It is one of the oldest breeds of domesticated rabbit known to man—records indicate it was well-known over a century ago. Secondly, the lop reached such a high standard of excellence in the 1920s that many breeders of fancy rabbits refused to compete against it in the A.O.V. (any other variety) class. The situation became so acute that a decision was made to give the lop a class of its own.

Of the three lops that are bred and exhibited, the English lop is the most popular. It would seem that ear length is of primary importance, but this is not quite true. In fact, ear width and shape are slightly more important. A good length ear in the English lop exceeds 25 inches. 27 inches in length is exceptional. Coupled with length, the ears should have plenty of width and substance, giving

The Britannia petite is fine-boned and small, and unlike the American Polish rabbit, it is posed in an upright position as shown here. These are red-eyed Britannia petites.

An ermine or white rex rabbit. Rex refers to a type of coat that is short and looks and feels like plush. The guard hairs are only as long as the normal hairs.

A black rex rabbit.

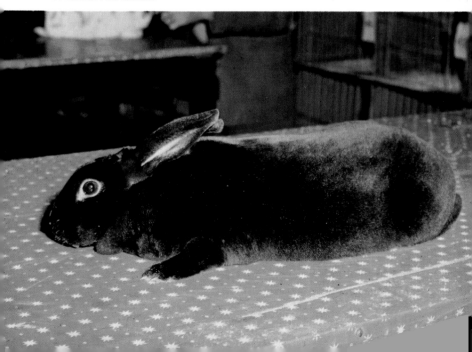

them a thick, leathery feeling. Good length is meaningless if the ears are very narrow and paper-like in substance. The ears should be well rounded at the tips and carried well. The carriage of the ears refers to the way they trail from either side of the head; they should not be carried erect.

When measuring the ears at shows, a wooden rule is always used, which reaches from ear tip to ear tip. A metal rule could cut the ears, possibly ruining a superb specimen. The ears must never be stretched, as the blood vessels lie close to the surface and any rupture would bruise the delicate tissue.

There is a controversy about the use of heat to increase the ear length in young stock. There has never been any definite proof, yet an excess of heat would certainly make the lop very uncomfortable.

The English lop is bred in a limited variety of colors: the most popular is sooty fawn. Others are black, fawn and marked varieties of these colors. The marked varieties must conform to a set pattern. The white patches on the head and nose must leave a butterfly smut of the color other than white. The white extends from under the chin and runs along the belly as in the tan and other varieties.

The lop type has massive proportions; the body is very mandolin-shaped, heavy and thick-set. The head is broad and bold and set well onto the shoulders. To complete the bold look, the eyes must also be bold and bright and as large as possible. The lop should be firm in flesh—not baggy or skinny.

Well known in Europe, the French lop was reportedly produced by crossing the English lop with an unknown breed. The French lop is a massive, thick-set breed with a wide, deep body. The flesh is firm and well-muscled, the bone heavy and strong. It is a short and cobby breed with a distinct curve from the nape of the neck to well-rounded loins and hindquarters.

The head is wide and bold, held on a short, thick-set neck. The ears, which are 12 to 15 inches long, are much shorter than on the English lop. The ears form a ridge on the crown of the head adding to the boldness and distinctive head shape. Drooping from the crown, the ears lie close to the cheeks in a horse-shoe fashion. Ear width and shape are also important in the French lop.

As in the English lop, the French lop pelt should be dense and soft, with no inclination to harshness or fly-back. The most popular color of the French lop is agouti, but any color is permissible including the marked pattern of the English lop.

The third type of lop is the dwarf. This is a rather new breed that originated by crossing the French lop with a dwarf. Although the dwarf breed has never been ascertained, it is probably the Netherland dwarf because the dwarf lop was produced in Holland, the home of the Netherland dwarf.

The dwarf lop is almost a miniature of the French lop, except that the dwarf weighs three and a half to four pounds when adult. The type required is exactly the same as for the French lop.

The usual color of the dwarf lop is agouti, but it can be bred in self black, white and sooty fawn. There are also two shoulder spots on either side of the body, but there must be no other white markings on the back and sides.

THE NETHERLAND DWARF

The Netherland dwarf is the miniature of the rabbit fancy. What it lacks in size, it makes up for in popularity. It makes an ideal pet for small children. Although the breed is noted for its bad temper, especially among the bucks, the adult dwarf doe is a most docile animal and usually makes a grand pet.

The advantages of rearing such a small breed are obvious: the amount of space needed to house a good-sized stud is minimal; feeding costs can be kept in proportion; and handling is a much easier task for the novice. A dwarf must never be handled by the ears, which are not large enough to get a good grip on when lifting the animal unless the weight is supported by the free hand.

The Netherland dwarf is quite a recent addition to the fancy rabbit fraternity. It came from Holland about 1947 or 1948. Although its origin is somewhat unclear, it is reported that the dwarf was produced by crossing a small wild rabbit with the dapper little Polish, which was very popular just prior to the Second World War.

It was quite well-developed before being exported to England, where it was taken to heart by thousands of fanciers. However, it was not until 1969 that the dwarf was seen on American shores.

A white rex rabbit.

A black rex rabbit.

A Dalmation rex rabbit. The spots should be distributed throughout the body but a smut must not be present.

A fawn rex rabbit.

Here, too, it was welcomed with open arms and soon became one of the most popular fancy rabbits.

The ideal shape of the dwarf is that of a round ball. A long body detracts considerably from the short, cobby type called for in the standards; therefore the most points are allotted to type.

The head should be as round as possible and as wide as it is long. Many very good specimens appear almost flat-faced because they excel in broadness of the skull. The ears should not be more than two inches in length. They should be carried erect, though they need not touch all the way up as they do in the Polish. They should, however, be rounded at the tips and well-furred. Any crossing of the ears is a serious fault and is called scissor-eared. The eyes are perhaps the most appealing feature of the dwarf. They should be as round as possible, big and bright. The body should be short and cobby, with no inclination to be racy or long in barrel.

On the exhibition table, the dwarf should pose similar to the Polish rabbit. The dwarf should not sit bolt upright, but should certainly keep its head and shoulders clear of the table to show off these points to the best advantage. Some schools of thought believe that the dwarf should not pose at all. But posing comes naturally to the dwarf and it should not be discouraged if it adds to the attractiveness of the breed. Young dwarfs can be taught to pose, but they should never be bullied during training or they will become nervous on the judging table and be difficult for the judge to handle. The dwarf bone is fine. The straight, short front legs make the controversy over posing more complicated. With short front legs, it may be difficult for the dwarf to sit well. Yet, if the legs are in proportion to the size of the body, there should be no problem.

Another attractive feature of the dwarf is the beautiful quality and texture of the coat. In this regard it is comparable with the best fur rabbits. The fur should roll gently back when stroked against the lie of the coat, returning to its natural position slowly and deliberately. Thin-coated dwarfs have a harsh coat which is inclined to be flyback.

The novice who desires a rabbit that is bred in a wide spectrum of colors can not do better than the dwarf. It is bred in almost every color and pattern known in the domestic rabbit. The most popular perhaps, is the red-eyed white. The color of the red-eyed white should be white as driven snow. Any yellow cast or stains should be avoided. Only regular cleaning of the hutch will keep the red-eyed white dwarf in a good condition for showing. Although the blue-eyed white is much less popular than its red-eyed counterpart, it is seen occasionally.

The next most popular color is the sable in either Siamese or marten pattern. The Siamese sable is a shaded self as is the smoke pearl Siamese, its recessive counterpart. The marten is a patterned sable that carries the tan pattern replaced by white. White hairs in the Siamese sable are a fault. They occur mostly on the undersides of all four feet, under the arm pits, on the chest and occasionally on the body and on the underside of the tail. It is allegedly the use of red-eyed whites in the sable breeding pen that causes these white hairs. The most common fault in the sable is lack of length and depth of the saddle. A good saddle should begin at the nape of the neck or just behind it. In poorly marked specimens the saddle does not begin until half way down the back; instead of gradually shading to the flanks, it stands out in contrast to the sides of the animal. In marten sables, the circle of white around the nose is often frosted, which indicates the presence of white hairs around the edge of the circle, giving the nose marking a smudged look.

In all other colors the dwarf compares favorably with similarly marked rabbits of other breeds. The Himalayan, which is the newest of these colors, is constantly being developed with regard to nose markings, stockings and density of color in the points. Early specimens were badly colored on the points and often had bad dwarf type. Although it would be impossible to detail all the known colors of dwarf, those mentioned are the most popular and those most often seen at exhibitions.

Early dwarfs were somewhat hard to breed; this was perhaps largely due to the small size of the doe which resulted in difficulty in passing her young at birth. The problem has been overcome and the dwarf is now usually a free breeder. Another fault in the earliest dwarfs was malocclusion of the front teeth which caused the teeth to cross (misaligned) and in some cases grow out from the front of the mouth. Although it has nearly been eliminated, it does appear occasionally in specimens that excel in head shape and broadness.

A blue rex rabbit.

A lilac rex rabbit.

A chocolate rex rabbit. This variety is known as the Havana rex breed in England.

A sable rex rabbit.

THE NEW ZEALAND BLACK

The New Zealand was produced in the United States as a utility animal. The meat qualities of this breed surpass all others. In addition, the fur is of such high quality that it can be used by furriers.

The latest color to be produced, the black, has the same meat and fur qualities as its earlier counterparts and is also rapidly becoming popular as an exhibition rabbit. The color should be jet black right down the fur, with no rusty or brown tinge. The toenails should be dark blue. White toenails are a total disqualification. The origin of the New Zealand black is unclear as little has been written about it.

THE NEW ZEALAND RED

The New Zealand red is perhaps the most popular as an exhibition rabbit. This is certainly true in the United States where it originated. The red was reportedly developed by crossing golden fawn sports with a cross of the Flemish giant and the Belgian hare. Although it has never been proven conclusively, it is now the accepted theory. Years ago a rabbit similar to the New Zealand red, but called the old English red, could be found in England. Although the old English red is extinct, two contemporary rabbits are very similar: the "Fauve de Bourgogne" in France and the "Fulvo di Burgogna" in Italy.

The actual color of the New Zealand red is known in horsebreeding circles as sorrel. It is not as deep as chestnut nor as light as the tan rabbit. If the red is too dark it is inclined to be rather untidy; if it is too light, it is more yellow than red. The only white allowed in the red is that on the underside of the four feet and also under the tail. Because the fur is apt to be thin around the eye, it gives a distinct eye circle impression. However, it is not a true eye circle. The eyes are hazel colored and the toenails are dark.

THE NEW ZEALAND WHITE

The original New Zealand white was believed to have come from the shores of that country. The New Zealand white is an albino and therefore free of all colored pigmentation. One of the most desirable characteristics of the white is the rapid growth rate of the newly-weaned youngsters, which makes them very popular as a commercial meat rabbit as well as a good laboratory rabbit.

Many large white rabbits are mistaken for New Zealand whites because of their size. All the New Zealand breeds have a rather harsh coat that resembles flyback features when stroked.

THE PALOMINO

The palomino is exclusively an American-bred utility rabbit. It was produced by Mark Youngs of Washington from a mixture of other breeds with the object of rearing a distinctly colored rabbit that would breed true genetically.

The palomino is bred in two colors—lynx and golden. The golden is a brilliant gold with a white to creamy undercoat. The coat has evenly dispersed light gold guard hairs. The belly, eye circles and underside of the tail are also creamy white. The top color and belly color should meet in a gradual shading on the flanks. This shading should be minimal and should not extend too much up the sides of the body. The eye color required by the standard is brown or hazel; any other eye color is a disqualifying fault. The toenails should be dark; white toenails are also a disqualification.

The palomino lynx is bright orange with a pure white undercolor. The whole coat is evenly ticked with lilac-colored hairs, giving the coat an attractive two-toned look. The ticking is one of the biggest failings in palominos; it should be evenly distributed, neither too light nor too heavy. If the ticking is too light, the two-toned effect is completely lost. If it is too dark, the coat tends to have a blue cast, which is a fault. The effect required is a silvering. White patches on any part of the body are a total disqualification. As in the golden palomino, the eye color should be brown or hazel and the toenails dark. Any other eye color or white toenails are also a disqualification. The ideal weight is nine pounds in bucks and ten pounds in does. The registration weight is eight to ten pounds in bucks and nine to eleven pounds in does.

THE POLISH

The Polish rabbit is referred to as "the kingpin" of the rabbit world. It is one of the most popular of the smaller breeds of rabbit both in England and the United States. The origin of the "Pole" is

A seal rex rabbit.

A chinchilla rex rabbit or "chinrex" as it is called by some fanciers.

An opal rex rabbit.

A lynx rex rebbit.

unclear, but it is known that it was first bred in Holland. Initially, it was probably a Dutch albino weighing about four to five pounds. The modern Pole should weigh two and one half pounds. Likewise, the origin of the name has never been established. It may not relate   at all to the country of Poland, as the Polish rabbit is rarely seen there. Perhaps, instead, the name was derived from polish as "to clean or shine," for this more aptly describes the rabbit.

In the early years of its development, the Polish was considered a utility rabbit and was regarded as something of a luxury at the restaurant table. During the war years many Polish were bred in backyard hutches as a meat source. The first Polish to be exhibited were albino. Records indicate that a class of 17 was shown at Hull in England about 1884.

The albino or red-eyed white has been extensively bred in England. The present Polish bears little resemblance to its early cousins in regard to weight. The Polish is smart, fine and nimble, compact in body and neat in appearance.

Short and fine in texture, the coat lies close to the body. The flyback feature is very important in a good-coated Pole. Too much length in the coat gives a rollback appearance. The coat should not be unduly harsh, nor should it be too soft.

The English Polish rabbit has only recently been introduced into the United States. It now enjoys a seperate classification and is called the "Britannia petite" so that it will not be confused with the American Polish rabbit.

The American Polish has a short, fine, dense coat, but it does not lie as close to the body as its English counterpart does. Type is very important. The body of the American Pole is shaped similar to the Netherland dwarf. The head is somewhat rounded and the body is full with well-rounded hindquarters. The English Pole is much finer in every respect. The body is sleek and compact, sprightly in appearance.

When posing, the Pole should sit bolt upright with its head high, ears upright and close together. The head is bold with a brilliant ruby-red eye. The eye is also bold and should be as large as possible, with the rich red color adding the final touch. The standard for the English Pole states that the ears should not be longer than two and one half inches, fine and well rounded.

Common faults in the ears are pointed tips, bare edges and an inability to hold them together. Bent ears and oversized ears are also common failings.

An essential part of the Polish rabbit's general appearance is good sound condition. The red-eyed white Polish must be clean and pure white in color. A Pole that is stained under or has a yellow cast to the coat has very little chance of success on the show bench. Coat stains are the fault of the exhibitor. If the rabbit is not kept in a clean hutch, it quickly becomes stained and dirty. In addition to cleanliness, the coat should have a definite sheen to add that little bit of sparkle. The Polish should feel firm in flesh, not fat or too thin. The eyes should be bright, not sullen or pale. A Polish rabbit can have all of these attributes, yet if it is not fine in bone, it will not have the typical Polish look essential to the rabbit's makeup.

In recent years there has been so much interest in the colored Polish that good coloreds can compare favorably with the very best red-eyed whites. The pioneer breeders of the colored Polish confronted numerous problems. The coats of the early coloreds were much too soft and long, lacking a good flyback texture. The ears were much too long at first; they were often bent and they lacked fineness. Nearly all of the early colored Polish were too strong in bone, making them look stumpy and awkward compared to the established red-eyed white.

The blue-eyed Polish was one of the first coloreds to be seen on the show bench, quickly followed by sables and smokes. Later came the self colors of black and blue, then the Himalayan or Himpole as it is often called. The silver Polish is not often seen, but it does exist in some studs in England.

The Polish rabbit has much to offer the newcomer to the rabbit fancy. It is easy to house and does not take up as much space as many other breeds of rabbit. Because of its small size, the Polish is cheap to feed and fairly easy to handle. However, due to its sprightliness, it can be quite a handful for the inexperienced.

THE REXES
The rex rabbit is an entirely different variety from the normal-furred rabbits such as the chinchilla and the Beveren. The rex-

A castor rex rabbit.

A red rex rabbit.

Orange rex rabbit with a temporary label attached to the ear.

An orange rex rabbit.

coated rabbits have a distinctive velvety fur achieved by guard hairs that are the same length as the undercoat hairs. The fur length required in the standard is little more than half an inch. The vibrissae or whiskers are curly and much shorter than normal.

The rex is a utility rabbit; its meat properties are the same as the normal-furred breeds reared exclusively for meat. The rex, however, is bred mostly for its exquisitely soft fur that is much sought after by furriers.

Rex rabbits cropped up in litters many, many years ago, but they were considered runts rather than sports or mutations and were killed off as soon as they appeared. The introduction of the rex to the world of exhibition rabbits is usually credited to Mssr. M. Gillet, a Frenchman who first exhibited this new mutation. However, in 1919 D. Callion, another Frenchman, experimented with the rex and found that the rabbits bred true. Mssr. Gillet continued with his experiments and bred the first castor rex to be exhibited anywhere in the world.

All the rex varieties are of the same type—a rather graceful rabbit gently sloping up to well-rounded hindquarters. The bone is medium strong, the head is broad and bold with the ears held erect. A small dewlap is permissible, but it must be in proportion to the body size and well-rounded. Between six and eight pounds is the acceptable weight. Heavier rabbits tend to look awkward and do not conform to the standard.

Perhaps the most popular of all the rex types is the ermine rex. This variety quickly came to the fore when it was first introduced into the rex standards. The ermine is well known for the density of its coat. It is very rare indeed to find one that is thin-coated like that of other colors. However, some ermines tend to be harsh in texture, which holds them back on the show bench. The color, of course, is pure white. Here again the ermine faces a handicap: if the color is tinted with a yellow cast, it does not stand a chance in good competition. A good, clean, healthy ermine rex is a really beautiful rabbit that is often at the top of the table when the awards are handed out.

Another popular color is the black, which is very much sought after by furriers. It has been found that pelts from this color match well. Unlike the ermine, the black formerly suffered considerably from lack of density in the coat. This has now largely been eliminated, but occasionally a thin-coated specimen does turn up. One of the most important aspects of the black rex is that it must be absolutely sound in color. It must be kept on clean bedding to avoid a stained and dirty underside. There must never be the slightest trace of a white hair in the body. In the early black rex, white armpits were prevalent in many exhibits and they were tolerated because the variety was in its infancy. Today the standard of excellence is very high and such faulty exhibits would never be tolerated.

While the blue rex never suffered from lack of density in the coat, it has been a difficult task to maintain a level color. The head and limbs suffered badly, generally appearing much too dark. Due mainly to the perseverance of breeders, a much more satisfactory color level is being maintained. White toenails were once occasionally evident, but have been almost eliminated in the contemporary blues.

Although the lilac rex suffered from bad color in its early days, it is now very popular in England. Too many early specimens had a muddy appearance, with a few white hairs in the coat. A good lilac rex is very pleasing to the eye. The color was reportedly produced by crossing Havana rex with blue rex; lilac is a dilute brown.

The nutria rex has become relatively rare. It used to be very popular as the pelt is one of the best types for fur work. The color is a self golden brown with a pearl-gray undercolor. A common fault is a rusty tinge in the coat color. Nutria rex have occasionally turned up in litters of Havana rex.

The Siamese sable rex is the rexed version of the normal-furred Siamese sable. It is a beautiful rabbit, but one that is not as popular as its attractiveness merits. The Siamese sable is, of course, a shaded self with a rich sepia-colored saddle over the back, shading down to a rich chestnut color on the sides and flanks. The dark sepia face, ears and limbs make a very attractive rabbit. A common fault in the sable rex is the occurrence of white hairs in the saddle and in the ears.

There was quite a controversy over whether the dark Siamese sable rex was a distinct color from the normal Siamese sable rex. Its distinction has now been generally accepted and the dark Siamese sable rex has been named the seal rex. While the former

A castor rex rabbit.

A Havana rex rabbit (chocolate rex in the United States) of English origin.

A Californian rex.

A tri-color rex rabbit. This is a new variety.

A standard rex rabbit with broken color.

sable and the seal rex are the same in nearly every way, the seal is very dark and carries an almost black saddle rather than the sepia saddle of the sable. The shadings of the seal are slight and not much paler than the saddle.

In the same group of shaded selfs is the marten rex, which is the rexed version of the normal-furred sable marten. The marten also has the dark sepia saddle, but it is on the white belly, inside the ears, on the underside of the jowls and the triangle. The seal marten rex is the same genetic color, but the dark sepia is almost black as in the seal rex of the Siamese pattern.

The orange rex—the rexed version of the New Zealand red—is a very strikingly colored rabbit. In the United States it is known as the red rex and differs in one minor point. While the orange rex has shadings down the flanks to an almost white belly, the red rex is solid in color and has no shadings or white belly. This is also true of the difference between the English and American New Zealand reds. The underside of the jowls and the eye circles are also white in the orange rex. Barred front feet and any dark smudging of the orange color are faults that should be watched in the breeding pen.

Closely related to the orange rex is the fawn rex, which is a golden fawn color rather than deep, rich orange. The belly, underside of jowls and underside of tail are white as in the orange rex. The orange and fawn can be bred in the same litter and are catered to by the same club in England.

Although it is very rarely seen, the fox rex has been reproduced in all the four colors of the normal fur silver fox: black, blue, chocolate and lilac. The fur of the rexed fox has a tendency to be harsh, but it is an attractive pelt for furriers.

Although at one time it was very popular on the show bench, the opal rex has also recently suffered from lack of interest. This may be due to the fact that the opal lacks good density of fur even though the color is one of the most attractive of all the rex breeds. The top color is soft blue followed by an intermediate band of golden tan. The undercolor is dark slate blue. The belly is white as in the normal fur opal.

The lynx rex, like the opal rex, has the agouti pattern. The lynx rex has hairs of three colors; the base is white merging into a bright orange tipped with silver, producing the shot silver effect required by the standard. A common failing in the contemporary lynx rex is that the base color, which should be white, has a bluish tinge.

Perhaps the most popular rex color among fanciers and furriers is the chinchilla rex. Good pelts bring high prices on the market and they are always in demand. The base of the fur is a dark slate color topped by a band of white. The slate top color is evenly tipped with black and white producing the chinchillated effect. The "chinrex," as it is more often called, is noted for the number of faults that can occur. Often the intermediate band is too dark and the top color is lifeless and dull. Often the chest and flanks are too light and void of the necessary ticking. But the most common fault in chinrex is the number of guard hairs that protrude above the coat giving it a rough, uneven feeling. A really good chinrex is a pride to own and exhibit and is well worth the trouble it takes to breed to perfection.

The castor rex is the forebearer of all the current rex colors because it is, in fact, a rexed agouti. The early castor rex had very poor coats. In addition to being full of protruding guard hairs, their coats were thin and sparse and the rabbits suffered from colds and chills. The castor rex color is another very attractive combination of the agouti pattern. The base color is dark slate blue with an intermediate color of rich orange. The top color is a deep, rich, red chestnut. Poor specimens are too light in top color and cannot compare with their earlier counterparts. However, although the early castor rex excelled in color, they were inferior in the density of fur.

The cinnamon rex is the true agouti rex. It is a golden tan on top, with a light orange intermediate band on a blue undercolor. The belly is white as in the normal fur agouti. Cinnamon rex are very rarely seen.

Another scarce color and pattern is the harlequin rex, which is the rexed version of the normal fur harlequin. Chinchilla rex is often used in the makeup of the harlequin rex. This variety is making a comeback in England with the rise in popularity of the harlequin fancy rabbit. The pattern and coloring are exactly the same as in the former. The magpie version of the harlequin rex is very rare indeed and may, in fact, be on the verge of extinction. The harlequin was once known as the "Japanese," but why the name

New rex rabbits with broken color. These were developed in the
United States.

A Dalmatian rex rabbit. The varicolored spots should be scattered as evenly as possible on the white coat.

Samples of rex rabbit pelts prepared for the fur trade.

applied to this rabbit is a bit of a mystery. It has been suggested that the orange and black pattern of the black harlequin is representative of the pattern of the Japanese national flag, the "Rising Sun." In general the harlequin rex is a poor relation to the more popular rex breeds. The fur is often thin and full of guard hairs, the ears soon become bare and void of good covering. For the new fancier, the harlequin rex can be a real challenge, both in improving the general standard and in attempting to produce a rabbit with just the right pattern.

Another rex color that is rarely seen is the silver seal. This rabbit is the rexed version of the ever-popular silver gray fancy rabbit. There was a boom of silver seal rex in England just after the Second World War; since then they have died out and may even be non-existent. The silver seal is not considered to be useful as a pelt rabbit.

The Havana rex, like the normal fur type, is a rabbit that is always in demand. It is self colored, a deep, dark chocolate brown. In the United States it is known as the chocolate rex. The Havana has a very large following in England and is always in the forefront at the big shows. The fur trade considers the Havana to be the best money maker of all. The pelts can be used for a multitude of purpose; even an average pelt is usable. Like most rex breeds, the young Havana rex rabbits have to be kept for at least six months to see what the adult coat will look like. Of course this takes time and space, but the experienced breeder of Havana rex will know what he has at quite an early age.

The smoke pearl rex is the dilute of the sable rex both in Siamese and marten patterns. It is a delicately colored rabbit that is very attractive to both fanciers and furriers. In the Siamese smoke pearl the saddle is a dark gray and gradually shades down the flanks to a silver gray. The ears, face, legs and tail are all dark gray. The marten smoke pearl has the same delicate shadings as the Siamese, except the pattern of the tan is replaced by white. The marten is rarely seen, but the Siamese is thriving. The pelts from these colors are used for trim on more expensive furs, such as mink. Gloves, capes and stoles are usually made from the pelt of the smoke pearl rex.

The two final varieties of rex do not conform to the accepted meaning of rex. The first is the astrex with fur very tightly curled all over the body except for the face, ear and feet. The astrex, formerly bred in most self colors including blue, black, and the most popular—lilac—is rarely seen now. In its heyday, more than one astrex was presented to the judge after being prepared with such devices as curling tongs!

The other rex that is distinct from the majority bearing that name is the opposum rex. Produced by Mr. T. Leaver of Kent, England in 1924, it was bred from chifox rex, which are chinchillated fox rex rabbits. Woolly argentes were added to produce a unique silvering effect over the whole of the opposum rex pelt. The opposum rex has a coat that is about one and a half inches long. The base (about an inch long) is the main color of the rabbit. Although black was most popular, any color is permissible. This bottom inch forms a base for the top half inch, which is white. The whole coat stands upright at right angles to the skin—a very peculiar characteristic. The face, ears and feet are the color of the rabbit, not silvered. While the opposum rex is not as popular as it once was, it is still extensively bred.

THE DALMATIAN REX

The Dalmatian rex is a very popular breed on the European continent, especially in France. The basic coat color is white with colored spots or patches over the entire body. These spots should be evenly spread and can be black, blue, brown, orange, sooty fawn or any bi-colored combination of these colors.

The ears and eyes should match the body markings. Black ears and black eye circles are allowed in any color or color combination of the markings.

The general faults are the same as for all rex breeds. The only fault peculiar to the breed is the lack of colored spots or patches on the body. The body should have no evidence of a saddle, nor should there be any traces of a butterfly smut.

THE OTTER REX

A lesser-known breed, the otter rex is more popular in parts of eastern Europe. It has been revived in England to some extent, but it is nowhere near as popular as its beauty deserves.

A sable rabbit. The English version of the American sable rabbit is the Siamese sable.

A trio of rexes ready for judging. A World of Pets photo.

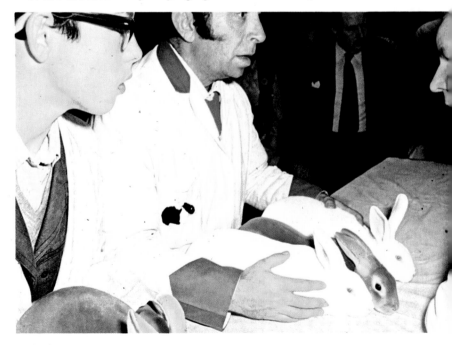

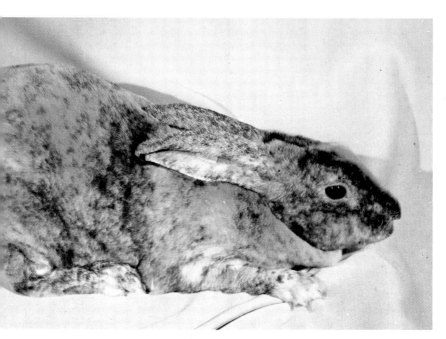

A harlequin rex rabbit.

A smoke pearl rex rabbit.

A Rhinelander rabbit bred in the United States.

Otter refers to the color of the rabbit's fur, which resembles the true wild otter. The top coat is a deep, dense black with an undercolor of slate blue. The belly fur is creamy white and extends under the chin and onto the underside of the tail. Between the black top coat and the cream undercolor, there should be a line of tan continuing along the hind legs.

The front legs should be self black. The chest is a mixture of black and tan, gradually merging with the other body colors. The nostrils and the nape of the neck are also tan-colored, but the eye circles and the inside of the ears should be fawn.

The type is like the normal rex and the faults follow the general pattern for all rex breeds. An additional fault is a rusty tinge in the top coat and the presence of white or tan hairs on the body except in the patterned areas.

THE RHINELANDER

The Rhinelander hails from Germany, as its name suggests. It is a well-known breed on the European continent and some specimens have found their way into the hands of English fanciers.

The Rhinelander is a dual-purpose rabbit with good pelt qualities and useful meat-producing assets. It was bred by crossing the butterfly breeds and the harlequin; little or nothing is known about its early development.

The general type is a meat rabbit with a solid, thick-set body and well-proportioned rump. The bone is medium strong with hind legs that are well muscled.

The ground color is white with a full butterfly marking of black on the nostrils. The eye circles are also black and completely encircle the eye. On the sides of the face there are distinct spots of black and yellow that should not run into the eye circles. The short, strong ears are colored yellow and black. Along the entire length of the back there is a saddle of colored spots somewhat similar to the English spot herring bone marking. Along the haunches and flanks are six to eight rounded spots of both colors—yellow and black. The fur is extremely dense and silky, about one inch in length.

THE MARTEN SABLE (Normal)

This rabbit is a fur breed that owes its name to its resemblance to the coloring of the wild marten. The marten sable appeared in litters of chinchillas just after the chin was first imported into England. Regarded as wasters, they were disregarded by the early fanciers. It was not until about 1919 that the sable was recognized as a distinct variety. Tom Leaver, of opposum rex fame, and David Irvine, the Southport fancier, were among the first to breed marten sables.

The Sable Rabbit Club was not formed until 1927. Since then, the sable has made a tremendous impact on the popularity of the fur breeds in general. Like the early chins, the first sables were of very poor quality both in color and density of fur. The coats of these sables were thin and often had a tendency to be slightly flyback. The color was very poor; often the flanks were so pale as to be sandy, a far cry from the beautiful sables of today.

The marten sable is tan patterned; the tan is replaced by white in the marten. The American Rabbit Breeders Association calls the marten sable the silver marten sable and places the English marten sable in the same class as the English silver fox. The American silver fox is an entirely different variety.

A silver marten sable rabbit, or marten sable as it is known in England.

A marten sable rabbit with very distinct ticking on the chest and sides.

Close-up of a Siamese sable rabbit.

Siamese sable rabbits.

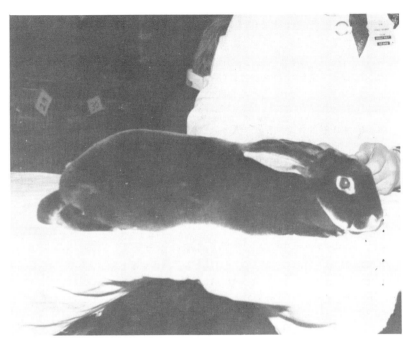

A marten sable rabbit ready for judging.

The marten sable was bred from the early chins and the Siamese sable was, in turn, bred from the marten. The general color of both varieties is the same. The body has a saddle of dark sepia brown extending from the shoulders to the rump. The saddle shades to light sepia on the flanks. The head, except for the ears, and the feet are also dark sepia.

The white markings of the marten are on the inside of the ears, the eye circles, belly, underside of the tail and under the jowl or jaw line. The chest is ticked with white as are the flanks, the rump and all four feet and legs. There is also a small triangle of white at the nape of the neck—this marking should be as small as possible, and is not really noticeable until the rabbit stretches its neck forward. There is also a border of white hairs around the nostrils. This is where the marten is most likely to be faulted; often these markings are smudged, which is termed "frosty nose." Sometimes the white hairs extend a little way up the nose. Very soft and silky in texture, the marten's fur is also thick and dense, about one to one and a half inches long.

The medium-sized marten should be neat and cobby. The back is very slightly arched with well rounded rump and hind quarters. According to the English standard, the ears should be small, neat and carried erect. Many marten sables fail on the ears, which are often much too long and wide with spoon-shaped tips that give the ears too much weight, causing them to hang on either side of the head similar to lop fashion.

THE SIAMESE SABLE

The Siamese sable is nearly the same as the marten sable except for the color and pattern. The type is exactly the same as the marten, with medium length of body and slightly arched back. The fur of the Siamese sable is also silky and dense. The Siamese sable is often considered the better fur rabbit of the two, but this is debatable. However, it is true that the Siamese is more popular. The Siamese carries markings similar to the Siamese cat.

The shadings of the Siamese sable are much more distinct than those of the marten sable. The Siamese is bred in three shades—light, medium and dark sepia. The light variety has better shading. The saddle, face and ears should be dark sepia, shading down to very light sepia on the flanks and belly. The medium

A Siamese sable rex rabbit. Note its dense and rich-looking fur, which is also beautifully shaded at the extremities.

231

A chocolate silver marten rabbit.

A black silver marten rabbit.

A blue silver marten rabbit.

A white satin rabbit bred and shown in the United States.

An ivory or white satin rabbit. The satin is medium in size and an all-American breed. Being meaty and not heavy-boned, they are popular with meat processors.

This white satin doe at the age of six months won the Best of Show award. Photo by Audrey Smith.

variety is slightly darker sepia but the shadings are less marked. The dark Siamese sable is almost self colored. The points are still noticeable, but to a lesser degree than either the light or medium shades.

In the United States, the dark sable is known as the "sable" and the medium and light Siamese are known as the Siamese sable.

The American sable is a few pounds heavier than the American Siamese sable. This may be due to the fact that the sable has been crossed with other breeds to obtain an even darker color. The Havana has been used very successfully for this purpose.

THE SMOKE PEARL

The smoke pearl, a dilute sable, was bred from sables about 1920. Originally known as smoke beige, the name was changed to smoke pearl in 1932. The color is an attractive light pearl gray and beige. As with the sable, the smoke is bred in Siamese and marten patterns. In both these types, the saddle of smoke color covers the whole of the back, from the nape of the neck to the base of the tail, shading off to a pearl gray beige on the flanks.

The marten smoke is ticked with long white guard hairs on the chest, flanks, rump and feet. The belly fur is white. The inside of the legs, inside of the ears, underside of the jowl and triangle are also white following the tan pattern.

234

THE SATIN

The satin is an all-American mutation of fur rabbit. It was first bred by Walter Huey of Indiana from a white doe and an English imported Havana buck. The resulting litter contained satin Havanas that were instantly recognizable because of the shiny appearance of their coats.

The satin has a high gloss sheen over its entire fur, resulting from the flattened scales of each strand of hair and the absence of the central hollow cells of the normal fur. From every angle, the fur of the satin displays the unique satin-like sheen that is so attractive.

Discovered in 1930, the satin mutation was not exported to England until about 1947. The most popular color of the satin is ivory, which is the white or albino. The actual color of the ivory is more creamy than white. Many other colors of satin are really the normal colors and normal markings of the fur breeds that have been satinized.

The American satin varieties include the black, blue, Californian, red, chinchilla, chocolate, copper, Siamese and, of course, the ivory. The copper and the Siamese are slightly different from those of the normal fur breed. The copper is similar to the Belgian hare in color, including the black ticking. The Siamese has a white base at each hair so the shadings are much lighter than in the normal fur Siamese sables.

The satin is a medium-sized rabbit weighing from six to eight pounds, with a cobby body and slightly arched back. The head is broad and carried on a short neck; the ears are in proportion to the body, wide and well-covered.

The satin bone is strong and powerful with front legs carried straight. The most important feature is the coat, which should be exceedingly dense, about one and a quarter inches in length. Although the satin pelt has been used in fur work, it is not as successful as was initially expected.

SIBERIAN

The Siberian was produced in England about 1930. Although its ancestry is unclear, it probably owes much to the self-colored English and the English spot. The motivation behind the produc-

A black satin rabbit.

A blue satin rabbit.

A chocolate satin rabbit.

A copper satin rabbit.

A red satin rabbit.

tion of the Siberian was the desire for rabbits that would provide matching pelts. Although the pelt of the Siberian is attractive, it is not used much in the fur trade today.

Many years prior to the introduction of the contemporary Siberian, a Himalayan-pointed Angora carried the name Siberian. This breed is certainly extinct now. The present-day Siberian, a fur breed, is slowly making a comeback in England after years of obscurity. The fur is rollback and extremely dense. It is described in the English standard as "blanket", which indicates that the undercoat completely covers all the guard hairs when the fur is pulled toward the head. The fur is approximately one inch in length and very soft in texture.

THE SILVER

The original color of the silver was silver gray. While controversy surrounds its origin, the silver was probably brought to the Western world by the early Portuguese sailors from Siam or India. A conflicting report indicates that silver grays appeared in litters of wild rabbits in Lincolnshire, England. These rabbits were known by a variety of names including Lincolnshire spriggs, millers, or Lincolnshire silver grays.

The first silver grays were used extensively for their meat and fur and a thriving industry sprang up in England in the early 1840's.

The silver gray is different from other breeds of rabbit in both texture and color of coat. The coat is black with a blue-black undercolor, evenly interspersed with silver-white guard hairs. The silvering results from the loss of pigmentation in the secondary guard hairs. The silvering provides a beautiful, sparkling appearance that makes a very attractive rabbit.

Following the silver gray, the silver fawn made its appearance in England. The silver fawn was originally a foreign breed belonging to the same family as the argente creme. It was known in France for some time before English fanciers became aware of it. The first silver fawns came from a litter of silver gray. After much experimentation, the color was perfected and became very popular as a fancy rabbit.

The third color of the silver is silver brown, produced by cross-

ing the silver gray with the Belgian hare. This was reportedly accomplished by a fancier from Kettering in Northhampton, England. The significance of the discovery was immediately recognized and the silver brown was nursed until it reached a satisfactory depth of color and even silvering. In England and the United States, the most popular silver is silver gray, followed by silver fawn and silver brown. A silver blue has become extinct from lack of interest by breeders.

The silver is a cobby rabbit, well-proportioned and very firm in flesh. The head is short, the ears short and well set on. The undercolor is very important if the top color is to be level and even. In fawn, the undercolor should be deep, bright orange; in browns a deep, rich chestnut color with a blue-black base.

The silvering should be bright and even over the whole body including the legs, feet, ears and chest. The majority of silvers fail in color in these areas. The amount of silvering determines whether the rabbit is dark, medium or light in color. The medium color is generally accepted as the breeder's main objective. Sharpness of silvering is also very important. The hairs should resemble new silver rather than white and should be a complete contrast to the ground color of the rabbit. The silvering should neither appear as patches nor should it be so sparse as to be unnoticeable. Young silvers do not have silvered coats until they reach the age of two to three months. The silvering is first noticed on the feet, head and ears and gradually works its way over the entire body by the time the young silver is five months of age.

The quality and texture of the coat are very important; it should be short and fully flyback. It is sometimes said that if you listen very carefully you can hear the coat of a good silver as its springs back into position when stroked against the lie of the fur. Although this description may seem exaggerated, it gives some idea of the requirement.

THE SILVER FOX

In America the silver fox is known as the silver marten. The fox was produced by crossing the black and tan rabbit with the chinchilla rabbit. The result is a fur rabbit with the coat qualities of the chinchilla breeds but marked with the pattern of the tan with loss of yellow pigment. The loss of yellow pigment means that the

A Siamese sable satin rabbit.

A chinchilla satin rabbit.

A Californian satin rabbit.

A Siamese satin rabbit.

A black silver marten rabbit. The silvery effect is produced by silver tipped guard hairs dispersed between the black hairs of the coat.

markings are white in color. This is a very popular fur rabbit. Perhaps the most important factor in the fox is the coat; it is allotted 40 points. The general fur length is about one inch, exceedingly soft and dense. The second most important consideration is color, which should be sound in all respects and of good depth. The type is a medium-sized rabbit with gently rising back. The head is wide and of medium size, ears of medium length in proportion to the rest of the rabbit.

The first color of fox was the black, then blue, chocolate and lilac. All these colors are seen at shows; it would be difficult to say which is the most popular.

THE AMERICAN SILVER FOX

The American silver fox bears no resemblance to the English version of the same name. The American fox is really a larger breed of silver. It was produced by crossing silvers with self-colored checkered giants by W.B. Garland of Ohio. In 1925 the breed was officially recognized and given its own standard.

The body is broad, with a slightly arched back on well-filled hindquarters. The body is of medium length, carried on legs that are straight and of medium bone. The head, which is bold and well-set on a short neck, bears a resemblance to the silver. The ears are short and carried erect. The fur is dense and about one inch in length. In both black and blue, the whole body is covered with silver guard hairs as in the silver.

THE TAN

The tan rabbit was bred by chance in a warren containing a mixture of wild and domesticated rabbits by the Rev. Cox in the grounds of Culland Hall Brailsford, Derbyshire, England. It was stated that the dam was a Dutch and the sire a wild agouti, but this has never been verified. Since the appearance of the first tans about 1880 the breed has become very popular.

The early tans were of very poor quality; it was not until many years later that progress could be detected in the depth of top color and tanning. These early tans were also rather bulky in shape and noted for their bad tempers—a total contrast to the tans of today, which are inclined to cobbiness and very docile by nature.

Gradually the breed began to take shape, keeping pace with color improvement. Much later, the blue tan was produced by Mr. A. Atkinson of Huddersfield, England. Atkinson reportedly crossed a black tan with a sooty fawn and then mated the resulting litter together, producing a mixture of black tans and blue tans. The blue became almost as popular as the black and rapidly made progress with the knowledge that was gleaned from the development of the blacks. Following the blues came the chocolates, and then the lilacs.

The tan standard states that the top color be dense and sound without any white or foreign color. This applies to all four colors. The tanning should be rich tan, deep and bright, extending from the underside of the jaw to the triangle at the nape of the neck, right down to the underside of the tail. The inside of the nostrils are also tan colored, but the color should not invade the face. The tan chest should join the underside of the chin and continue in a line along the jaw to the triangle behind the head. The belly is also tan colored; the color extends down the inside of the front legs, but not onto the front of the feet or the foot pads, which are usual-

A silver gray rabbit.

A young silver gray rabbit. Silvering must be present throughout the body, including the legs and ears.

A silver brown rabbit.

A silver fawn rabbit.

A chocolate and tan rabbit. Tans are small rabbits weighing only between four to seven pounds.

ly white. This is not a fault and should be disregarded. The outside of the front legs are densely colored in the same color as the rabbit. The toes should be tan on top—a point which is often overlooked. The hind legs and feet are also tan colored on the inside and colored according to the color of the top coat on the outside. The demarcation line along the leg should be straight and even, dividing the outside toe from its fellows, leaving this toe tan colored and the others black, blue, chocolate or lilac.

The eye circles are tan, but the amount of tan should only be a very thin line around each eye. The ears are colored like the body on the outside and tan colored on the inside. There should also be an edging of tan around each ear.

The general type of the tan should be similar to the Dutch from which it is supposedly evolved. The body should be short and cobby without any inclination to raciness. The ears should be as short as possible, held erect in the fashion of the wild rabbit. Condition plays a very important part of the general appearance of the tan. A

black tan that is in tip-top condition should really shine like polished ebony. This also applies to the three other colors; each should have that beautiful glossy finish to the coat. It was once thought that tans would make good pelt rabbits, but it has never been successful.

THE THURINGER

This also is a rabbit that is very popular in parts of Europe but not often seen elsewhere. Consistent with many of the breeds from this part of the world, it can be classed as a dual-purpose rabbit. It is extensively exhibited on the European continent and also makes a very useful meat rabbit. The Thuringer reportedly originated in Germany where it was bred from crosses of the Himalayan, argente and possibly the Flemish giant.

The type is a medium- to large-sized rabbit, thick-set and rounded in shape. The back is strong with well-rounded haunches. The head is wide and well set on to the short neck, the ears are wide, but the length is in keeping with the size of the body and head.

The color of the Thuringer is very similar to the sooty fawn or tortoiseshell. The ground color is, perhaps, a shade darker than the former and is described in the English standard as buff. The entire coat is evenly covered with dark-colored guard hairs, giving an appearance of chamois leather when blended with the dark top coat. The points, which include the face, eye, circles, ears, feet, and tail are all bluish black colored. The haunches are also covered with a bluish black shading which should blend into the yellow very gradually. The whole coat is very dense and silky.

A black silver fox rabbit. The other variety of this exclusively American breed is the silver fox.

A silver fox rabbit bred in England. In the United States the English silver fox is known as the silver marten.

A blue silver fox rabbit from England.

One correct method of holding a rabbit. It is grasped by the base of the ears and the rump is also supported.

Management

Good management is essential if the rabbitry is to be run in an efficient manner. The main ingredient of good management is regularity—it is threaded through a whole multitude of jobs that must be performed to keep the rabbitry clean and in good order. Good livestock management is not acquired overnight. It comes with practice and experience. Trial and error play an important role in learning how to look after a rabbitry.

An old saying—"one man's meat is another man's poison"—is somewhat applicable to livestock management. What suits one breeder and his rabbits may be detrimental to another breeder and his rabbits. Everyone has his own method for doing things, even the simplest tasks such as feeding and cleaning. The right way to do things is the way that suits you; other fanciers can be imitated to a certain extent, but not in all instances. Although experience is the best teacher, there are certain rules that every manager should observe.

The fancier who takes time and trouble with his stock will generally be more successful than the fancier who rarely has the time to make sure his stock is well cared for. Cutting corners is useless. There is no shortcut on the long and sometimes frustrating road to success. Even when the fancier attains success, he cannot allow himself to sit back and enjoy the fruits of his labor. He must be forever on the alert in order to keep his stock fit and at their best.

One of the rabbit fancier's greatest management assets is his instinct that tells him when everything is going right and when something is amiss. Handling the stock regularly sharpens this instinct. The breeder will learn to recognize when a rabbit is losing flesh, whether it is putting on too much weight or whether it needs a little more conditioning. Simply by looking over his stock,

an experienced fancier can tell whether a particular rabbit is fit and well or about to succumb to a minor illness. The best advice for a breeder is to keep the eyes and ears open and the mouth shut!

HANDLING

Rabbits must be handled regularly—at least once a week should be the rule. Certain guidelines apply to rabbit handling. Rabbits that are handled roughly will soon resent it and will quickly become wild. The hind feet of a struggling rabbit can inflict serious scratches on the handler. Yet, nine times out of ten, there is no reason for the rabbit to struggle at all if the simple rules of handling are followed.

Firmly but gently is the watchword when handling rabbits. There are numerous ways for a rabbit to be picked up. The most common method is to begin by lifting the rabbit with the aid of the ears. The rabbit is turned so that it is facing the handler. The right hand is placed around the base of the ears, grasping them firmly but gently. (The many tiny blood vessels in a rabbit's ears can be torn or badly bruised by rough handling.) The left hand is placed over the rabbit's rump. As the rabbit is lifted, the breeder's hand moves down the hindquarters and under the rabbit. Under *no* circumstances should the rabbit be lifted by its ears alone.

To examine the belly, the handler gently lowers the rabbit onto a table or bench and removes his left hand from underneath the rump. The rabbit's body is now balanced by the grip on the ears, with its weight resting on the table. The left hand, which is now free, is held parallel to the fancier's body and placed across the hind legs to prevent the rabbit from kicking out. The belly and sexual organs of the rabbit can then be inspected freely and without any discomfort to the rabbit.

Another method for handling rabbits is to place one hand around the base of the ears while the other moves under the body and supports all the rabbit's weight. A rabbit should be carried only a short distance in this manner, such as from one pen to another close by.

Larger rabbits can be lifted by grasping the loose skin over the neck and shoulders with one hand. The other hand encircles the rabbit's body and lifts it so that it can be carried under the

Manure which collects under the hutches is useful; it supports colonies of earthworms for bait or can be used for fertilizing gardens.

A small litter is not profitable to a commercial breeder. A doe is bred the most number of times in the shortest time intervals between births.

A Siamese smoke pearl rabbit.

A marten smoke pearl rabbit.

Method of picking up a small rabbit without holding the ears and causing damage.

handler's arms. This method requires considerable practice and can be performed only by a confident handler.

Smaller rabbits such as the Polish and dwarfs should never be lifted by the ears at all. The correct way to handle these breeds is to place one hand over the back and rump, the fingers grasping the rabbit's muscles on one side and the thumb grasping the muscles on the other. The rabbit can then be lifted easily and safely. There is no need to put pressure on the sides of the rabbit; indeed, much damage can be done to the internal organs if they are squeezed. This method is often used on the judging table by the pen steward. If the rabbit must be taken from a show pen by the steward, it should be turned so that it faces away from the steward. The rabbit can then be removed from the pen backwards. If it is removed as it faces the steward, it will spread its hind legs, which will catch the sides of the doorway of the pen, making it impossible for the rabbit to be removed without a struggle.

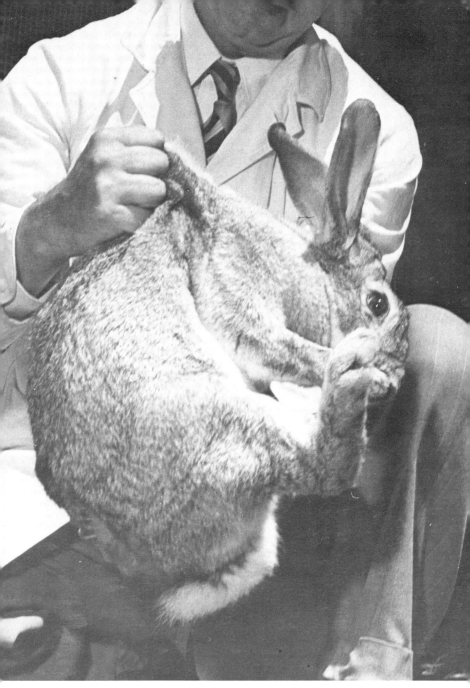

Another method of lifting a large rabbit without holding the ears; it is held by the shoulders and supported on the rear simultaneously.

Many wild mammals, including the European wild rabbit, have the agouti colored fur. However, this type of fur is seldom accepted for showing in many rabbit breeds. A black and tan rabbit (below). Tans are small rabbits that are known for their beautiful and lustrous furs.

A chocolate and tan rabbit.

An exhibition type of black and tan rabbit.

A lilac and tan rabbit.

INSPECTING RABBITS BEFORE PURCHASE

Whenever possible, the potential fancier should inspect his purchases before parting with his money. Because this is not always possible, the fancier sometimes must trust the honesty of the vendor. The rabbits still must be inspected upon arrival, however, to determine whether they are the correct sex and whether they carry any obvious signs of disease.

If the rabbits are unsatisfactory, the owner should be informed at once and arrangements should be made for the rabbit's safe return. Although it is impossible for a rabbit breeder to guarantee his stock for any length of time, sound, healthy stock should always be sent out. Stock that is ill or not up to the standard gives the seller a bad name.

The experienced fancier can learn a number of things from examining the rabbit. When inspecting rabbits before or after purchase, the ears should be examined meticulously for any signs of ear canker. Canker can be identified by a yellowish, strong-smelling discharge. There should be no signs of mange or other skin disease. The ears should be well covered with fur and quite clean.

The eyes of a sick rabbit will be dull and lifeless. If the rabbit suffers from an eye disease, they will produce a clear, watery discharge. The rims of the eyes will be red instead of the usual skin coloring. In the healthy rabbit the eyes will sparkle. They will be clear of any foreign matter and well colored.

A rabbit with a nasal discharge is usually suffering from a chill or cold. Avoid buying rabbits in this condition. It is extremely contagious and will spread throughout the rabbit shed in no time. The healthy rabbit's nose will be clean, the breathing will be easy and the nose will twitch constantly in the characteristic manner.

Inspect the fur all over the body, making certain there are no signs of mange or excessively loose fur. Exceptions can be made in the case of does that have littered recently as they will be scant of fur on the belly.

The legs and feet should be inspected thoroughly. Although it is a minor consideration, the nails of all four feet should be kept trimmed. The hocks on the hind feet should be well covered with fur, with no signs of sores or scabs.

While the sex of the rabbit is being determined, the organs should be inspected. Any sign of sores or discharge indicates the rabbit is suffering from hutch burn or rabbit syphilis.

The anus should be clear of any foreign matter. Caked fecal pellets in this area indicate that the bowels have been loose. This could be caused by nervousness, but it is best to be on the safe side and reject such rabbits.

SEXING RABBITS

The most reliable way of sexing rabbits is to examine the sexual organs. The rabbit is held as described earlier by balancing the body with one hand and keeping the head and ears steady with the other. The hand that holds the body is slipped from under the rabbit while it rests on a table or bench.

If the skin just in front of the organ is pulled slightly with the fingers and pulled from the tail end by the thumb of the same hand, the organ will be exposed and a positive identification can be made. If the rabbit is a buck, the penis will protrude and the testicles may also be evident. The adult buck in breeding condition will reveal a pair of brown specks on either side of the testicles. The doe will show a slit-like organ that will open up when very slight pressure is exerted. Generally, the vulva of the doe is nearer the anus than is the penis of the buck.

Young rabbits are sometimes difficult to sex until they reach eight to ten weeks of age. It is *possible* to sex newborn rabbits, but it takes much experience and a good pair of eyes to do this properly. If the baby rabbit is held in the palm of the hand, stomach-side up, with the head facing the handler's wrist, it can be sexed in the same way as adults. If the baby rabbit is viewed from the side, a more positive identification can be made. A magnifying glass is necessary for accuracy. Viewed from the side, the penis of the young male will be seen as a slightly rounded tip. Nipple spots will be evident in both sexes, so they are not a reliable guide to sex.

Although it is generally accepted that the adult buck has a broader head and is slightly smaller in body than the adult doe, this system is unreliable, as no two rabbits, even those born in the same litter, will be the same shape.

A trio of tan patterned rabbits. The tan color should be bright and limited to the areas specified in the standard. Photo by Ray Hanson.

In this standing position of a wild European rabbit the pale colored parts of the body are visible. These correspond to the areas that are colored tan in the tan rabbit breed.

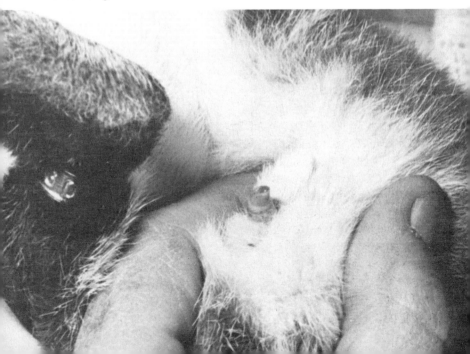

External genitalia of a female rabbit or doe.

External genitalia of a male rabbit or buck.

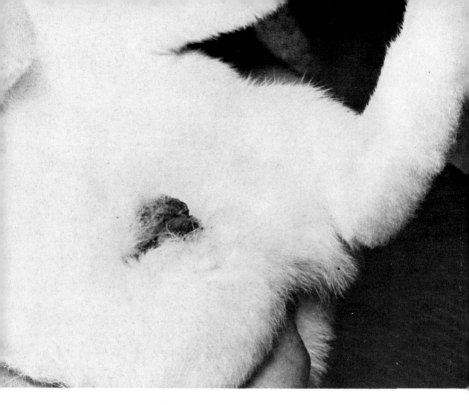

Rabbit with venereal disease.

The buck is in breeding condition when the testes have descended fully and are plainly visible. The doe is in breeding condition when the vulva is visibly red and swollen.

MOLT AND GROOMING

Molting is a natural process whereby the rabbit sheds its coat once each year and grows a new one at the same time. In most rabbits this is a quick and easy annual process that occurs without any trouble. However, there are rabbits that always stick halfway through the molt and remain in this unfinished state for quite some time. For the breeders of exhibition and pelt-producing rabbits, this is an annoying and time-consuming experience.

The molt begins over the back and progresses towards the rump and down the sides. At the same time, the feet, face and ears are molted. The molt travels down to the underside and tail, finishing on the chest.

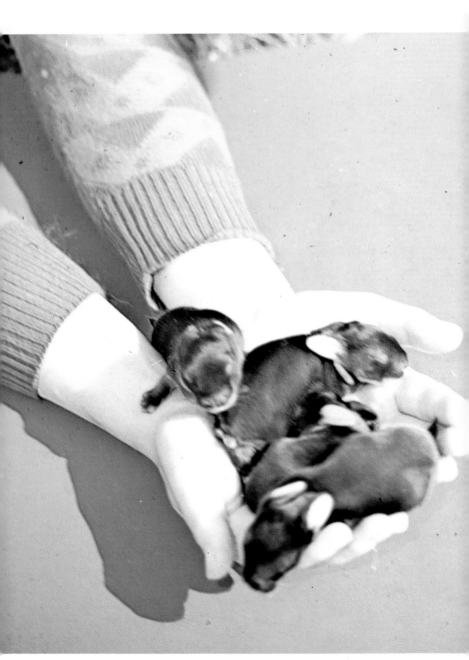

A handful of tans just four days old. Adults at most weigh only six pounds. Small breeds are economical—they need less food and space.

A tan rabbit at eleven days of age.

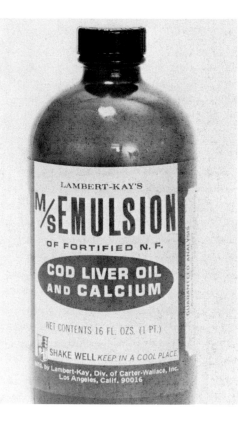

Cod liver oil helps in keeping the fur in good condition; it is especially needed during the molting season by rabbits that are maintained on non-pelleted food.

Regular grooming is essential if the rabbit is to get through the molt quickly and without trouble. The basic necessity is to keep the coat free from any dead hairs that might clog and slow up the process. Usually the bare hands are dampened with a little saliva from the fancier's mouth and used to rid the coat of these hairs.

The fancier's hands are placed over the shoulders and swept back over the backbone towards the rump. The hairs are collected on the hands and will stick if sufficient moisture has been applied to the palms. The whole coat should be groomed in this manner every day until the dead hairs are completely removed. Some rabbits will stick in the molt around the base of the ears. This can be hurried along by lightly gripping the ears with the palm of the hand facing the handler. The thumb of the same hand is used to stroke the fur in front of the ears. If this area is kept free of dead hairs, it will quickly molt and soon become presentable.

Various grooming aids are recommended. It is strictly a matter of personal preference on the fancier's part. A slightly dampened chamois leather, a fine-toothed comb or a soft brush can be used. In addition, specific molting aids are available. These include special foods rich in oils that heat the blood of the rabbit such as linseed, maize and various greenfoods like chickweed and shepherd's purse.

If linseed is used it can either be provided with the usual food or it can be steeped in cold water. After steeping, a jelly will form over the top of the seed. As much as possible of the jelly should be drained off and the remainder mixed with the seed and the normal rations to form a mash. This mixture should be fed to molting stock immediately after preparation, as it quickly becomes moldy.

Stock that is intended for exhibition should be groomed regularly even when not in molt. A good brushing will give a nice bloom to the coat. White rabbits should always be kept on clean white sawdust. The soiled portion should be removed whenever it becomes damp or dirty.

The rabbit's coat can be kept clean with a little talcum powder or corn flour. These substances should be rubbed into the coat well and then vigorously brushed out. An old-fashioned grooming aid is a dry crust of bread that is rubbed into the coat.

FEEDING

Feeding is discussed in detail in another chapter. But it is important to remember that regular feeding is part of the whole process of good management. A creature of habit should be fed at the same time each day. The feeding time depends entirely on the schedule of the fancier. Rabbits can be fed twice a day, but it is not really necessary if the rations provided are sufficient to maintain a full level of nutrition. Once a day is adequate.

A fancier with a large number of rabbits will work out a regular feeding routine to save himself time and trouble. It is foolish to walk from one end of the rabbitry to the other with a pot that must be replenished by walking all the way back to the hutch. Big commercial rabbitries use corn bins mounted on trolleys that can be pushed along as the stockman makes his way from one hutch to the next. The same system should apply to watering if the stock has to be fed by hand.

A litter of tans. A uniform progeny is one of the objectives of a breeder whether he breeds them for the meat market, the fur industry or for exhibition.

Good health of a rabbit or any other animal is reflected in part by the appearance of the eyes and condition of the fur. Note the alert, bright and clear eyes and clean coat of this young rabbit of undetermined origin.

FOSTERING

Fostering is the practice of taking a litter of baby rabbits from one doe and placing them into the nest of another doe for her to rear as her own.

Although this practice comes generally under the heading of breeding, it is a skill that must be mastered while learning about rabbit management.

There are many reasons for removing the newborn litter from a doe and placing them with another doe. In the case of the smaller breeds, this can be done effectively if an English or Dutch doe is mated at the same time as the intended foster doe. When the rabbits litter, they should produce their young within forty-eight hours of one another. The litter from the foster doe is humanely destroyed.

The litter from the breed doe is placed in the foster doe's nest after rubbing them all over with some sawdust from the foster doe's nest box. The litter should be left for about fifteen or twenty minutes to absorb the scent of the nesting material. The foster doe is then replaced in her hutch. She should not notice the change in the appearance of her litter and should proceed to rear them as though they were her own. The breed doe can then be mated again and a larger number of litters can be produced. The English and Dutch does make excellent mothers, as they have strong maternal instincts. They are bigger rabbits and can therefore stand the strain of rearing a large number of young in their litters.

This practice is also used whenever marked rabbits are reared. The litters are inspected at birth and the mismarked young are removed. Those remaining are put together with the litter of another doe of the same breed that has also had her litter graded.

CLEANING

The cleaning of the rabbitry is a job that needs to be done very regularly if a high standard of hygiene is to be maintained. It is perhaps the least desirable, but also the most important, of all the aspects of good management. If rabbits are not kept clean and comfortable, they can never remain healthy. As with feeding, a routine must be followed. Hutch dressing or bedding should be clean and free from dampness.

There are a number of choices for bedding material. The most popular is softwood sawdust, which should be white and unsoiled. Many lumber merchants are pleased to allow rabbit fanciers to help themselves to sawdust from under their saws. Sometimes there is a small charge, but it is worth the price if a regular supply of sawdust can be obtained. Wood shavings can also be used for bedding, but they are not as absorbent as sawdust. The best shavings are in the form of wood chips; they are usually blown or sucked from under the woodworking machines into another room, where they collect in a pile. One disadvantage is that rabbits will chew wood shavings while they rarely eat sawdust. Peat can also be used as a hutch dressing. It is not as absorbent as sawdust or shavings, but it does not smell and is easily obtained from any garden store. If the peat is too dry, however, it will give off a dust that can irritate the rabbit's eyes and nose.

Rex rabbits are sometimes bedded on legume straw—the stalks collected after the harvest. There are disadvantages to this type of bedding. Straw is not absorbent and is easily soiled. Rabbits will also eat straw. However, it will provide the rex rabbit with a soft cushion to rest on without fear of developing sore hocks.

Newspaper is sometimes used as a bedding material. A caution, however, is in order: the print is poisonous, and rabbits will chew paper. But paper is a warm substance and can be useful as lining for a nest box. For small-scale rabbit owners—and for some large-scale owners as well—the most sensible way to obtain good bedding is to buy the conveniently packaged products available in pet shops.

Once the bedding is soiled, it has to be removed to keep the hutch fresh and clean. The fancier who keeps only a small number of rabbits will be at an advantage, because he can merely dump the soiled bedding into the trash can. The larger rabbitry is faced with a weekly disposal problem. One solution is to locate a gardener or group of gardeners who will be glad to take the bedding for use as potting compost.

However, this is not a universal solution. For most fanciers, a suitable dump must be found. The bedding has to be put into bags of some kind. Empty grain bags can be used. Rather than throwing them away after the food has been used, the fancier can save the empty bags for bedding disposal. The bedding is emptied at

A Rhinelander rabbit. This German rabbit breed is both a meat and a fur breed.

A young Rhinelander rabbit and a guinea pig drinking from the same earthernware bowl.

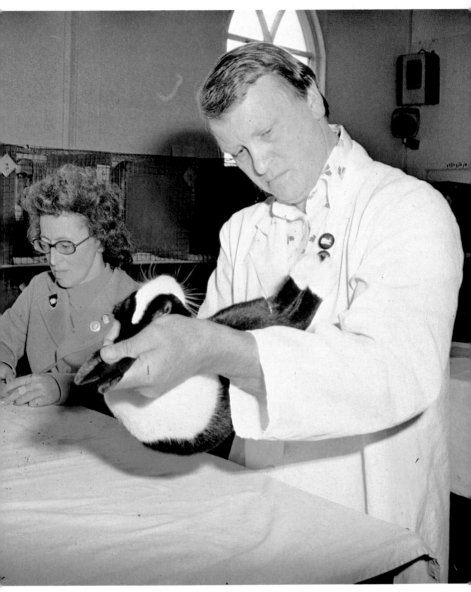

A judge in the process of examining a black Dutch rabbit in a rabbit show in England.

the dump and the bags are taken home for use again the next week.

As with all other aspects of management, cleaning should be done according to some sort of routine. Any labor-saving system is well worth consideration.

Cleaning should be done thoroughly every time. Replacing soiled bedding with clean bedding and leaving unsoiled bedding is not a good practice. This is functional only for white rabbits; even then it should be done every day and the entire hutch cleaned out during the weekend. In all other cases, all of the bedding should be removed once a week. The hutch should be thoroughly brushed out and all the corners of the hutch should be disinfected. Total disinfection is difficult, but it is important in limiting the risk of disease.

If the hutch has been occupied by a sick rabbit, the walls, floor and ceiling can be sterilized by running a burning blowlamp over all the surfaces. The hutch should then be left empty for at least a week to avoid reinfestation.

In all cases, fresh bedding should be placed in the hutch to a depth of at least one-half inch all over the floor. If the bedding is skimpy, the rabbits may develop sore hocks from stamping on the hard floor surface.

Once the cleaning is completed, the soiled bedding should be removed from the rabbitry as quickly as possible. The dirty bedding will attract flies and other vermin if it is left lying around for any length of time.

MANURE

Much of the manure produced by the stock of the rabbit breeder is thrown out with the soiled bedding. This need not be the case. There are many uses for the manure if the time and trouble are taken to extract it from the bedding.

The amount of manure produced by any rabbit will depend primarily upon the actual size of the animal. The larger breeds could produce as much as three hundred pounds per year. A breeding doe will, of course, provide much more. The smaller breeds will provide considerably less, but it can be farmed in the same way.

The time required to farm rabbit manure will depend on the way the rabbits are bedded. If the stock is kept in all-wire pens, the

problem of extraction solves itself, because the waste matter will simply fall through the holes in the wire, where it can be gathered up.

Rabbits that are bedded on straw will be useful for producing compost instead of manure.

The whole bedding can be dumped onto the compost heap, where it will rot down. Manure from rabbits that are kept on sawdust has to be strained and separated from the bedding. This is a long, arduous process and not a very pleasant chore.

An analysis of rabbit manure confirms the fact that manure farming can be an economically feasible proposition. Rabbit manure in its dry form contains roughly 1 percent potash, 2.7 percent nitrogen and 1.5 percent phosphoric acid. Much less fresh rabbit manure than cow or horse manure is needed to produce the same amount of dry manure. Estimates indicate that the cow and horse have to produce one and a half times more fresh manure than the rabbit to produce the same amount of dry manure. Dry rabbit manure can be ground and sold as fertilizer. The most practical use of rabbit manure for the fancier who gardens is to dig it right into the earth. Because rabbit manure is soluble, the contents will disperse quickly. There may be a shortage of nitrogen at first, but the balance will soon correct itself.

The most practical way to introduce rabbit manure into the ground is to dig a trench the whole length of the plot. The manure is placed at the bottom of the trench and the earth is replaced. As each trench is opened and filled, progress will be made across the plot.

Liquid manure can also be made very quickly. The manure is put into open-weaved sacks or bags and suspended in a barrel or tub of water. If the rabbitry roof has a gutter, the water pipe can be directed into a water butt and a sack of fecal pellets suspended in it. Liquid manure can be drawn from the barrel whenever it is required by fixing a tap at the bottom of the water butt. Some sediment will collect in the liquid manure and settle at the bottom of the butt. This can be strained away.

If the rabbit manure is applied right onto the compost heap, it should be covered with a layer of soil to discourage flies. A dressing of hydrated lime should also be applied in order to assist the rotting-down process and also to keep the heap sweet-smelling.

A rabbit when held correctly, like this Dutch rabbit being judged, feels comfortable and will usually not struggle.

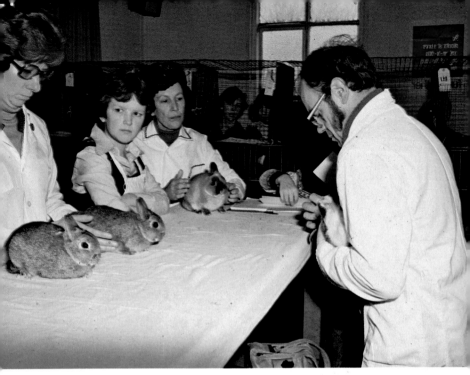

Netherland dwarfs being examined in a show in England.

At the same show another judge is examining the texture, density and condition of an entry's fur.

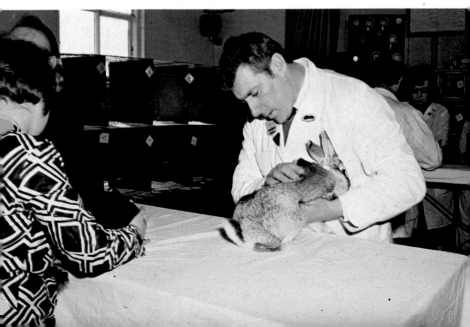

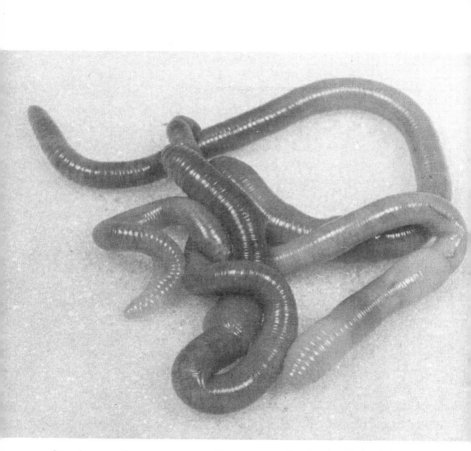

Specimens of a common earthworm species in the United States. These worms congregate naturally under rabbit hutches, attracted by rabbit droppings there, turning poor soil into valuable humus.

RAISING WORMS

The art of worm culture is perhaps practiced more in the United States than anywhere else in the world. The worms are bred in special beds placed below the rabbit pens. The beds are used only under outdoor pens. The bed is enclosed with wooden boards about one-inch thick and ten to twelve inches wide. The material for the bed can be either peat or very old sawdust. If sawdust is used, it must be at least ten years old and have lost all of its resin content.

The bedding is laid to a depth of at least six inches and dampened with water. The bedding must be damp, not wet; this is very important. When squeezed by hand, only a drop or two of water

should run between the fingers. The worms can be purchased as a special culture kit containing about one thousand worms.

The rabbit manure that drops from the hutches will be eaten by the worms and will turn into humus. The only requirement is that the bed be turned over at least once a week. The turning will ensure cleanliness and guard against offensive odors. The beds should be emptied at least once a year so that they are kept in good condition and to keep the acid content to a minimum.

For the worms to reproduce successfully, they must be kept in good condition at a suitable temperature. Earthworms are bisexual, producing egg packets that hatch after an incubation period of about twenty days. From each egg five to fifteen worms emerge, each about half an inch long. The young worms will reach maturity in about three months and they, in turn, will begin to breed.

When there is an appreciable amount of young worms in the bed, the manure on which they feed can be supplemented with some freshly mowed grass cuttings or other materials that will quickly rot down. The most commonly used worm in worm culture is the common red worm found in most garden soils. There are others native to tropical countries, but they require more heat and, therefore, are less hardy.

The worms can be sold as fishing bait, and the humus that the worms produce can be sold as potting compost. It is not necessary to sell any of these products. Their presence under the rabbitry will solve the waste problem and also keep the risk of bacterial infection at a minimum. But the sale of the worms and humus will somewhat offset the cost of running the rabbitry.

If the worms are sold as fishing bait, they should be packed in strong bags or containers which contain clean, moist peat.

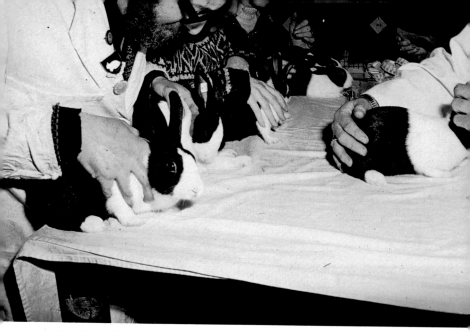

Dutch rabbits competing in an English rabbit show. Dutch rabbits are widely bred and are always popular in shows around the world.

As a rule spectators and rabbit owners are not allowed to approach the judging table during judging.

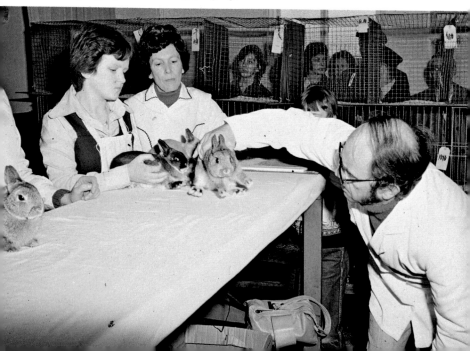

Shown are two views of the judging arena, where rabbits are being judged, at the Colorado State Fair held at Pueblo, Colorado.

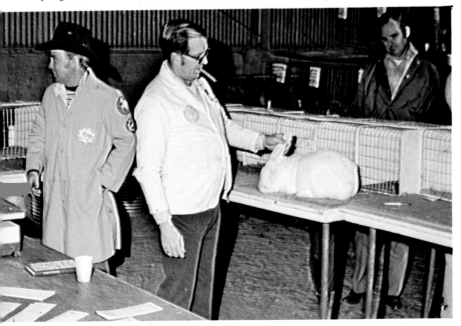

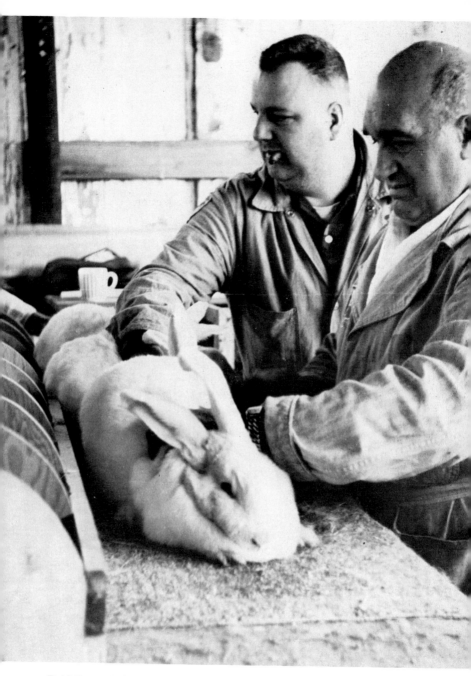

Rabbit meat classes are judged in meat pens. A meat pen consists of three rabbits of the same breed and variety. Disqualification of one disqualifies the rest.

Commercial Rabbit Production

Man has been raising rabbits for meat production for hundreds of years. All rabbit meat is edible. It is rich in protein and very easily digested. The meat obtained from the domestic rabbit is different from that of the wild rabbit. Domestic rabbit meat is more tender and carries more fat than that of the wild rabbit, which is inclined to be coarser and have very little fat.

There is no single breed of rabbit that is bred for its meat alone, because meat-producing rabbits are usually large and therefore provide very attractive pelts that can be utilized in some way. The rabbits used for their meat are not restricted to the fur breeds alone. Indeed, some of the fancy breeds make very good carcasses with very little dressing-out waste. Among the fur breeds, we can include the New Zealand, the ever-popular Californian and the chinchilla. The fancy breeds include the harlequin, the English and the Flemish, English and American giants. Neither listing is exclusive.

Correct management is extremely important in commercial rabbit raising. Because the profit margin is so thin, the accent must be on as little waste as possible in both time and money.

Among the breeds most frequently raised, growth rate is the prime factor in their selection. Time is precious to the rabbit raiser; therefore, the maximum use of the does should always be a prime consideration. The hutches or pens should be designed so that cleaning is not as laborious or as time-consuming as it would be for other rabbit breeders. The hutches normally used for commercial rabbit production are the wire pen type. These pens require very little maintenance, and bedding is not necessary. The fecal pellets from the rabbits fall through the wire floors and onto the floor underneath the pens, where they can be disposed of (or put to good use) without the usual rigors of cleaning.

A white red-eyed bunny. Pure red-eyed rabbits are born with pink eyes and lack a cornea. The iris becomes slightly pigmented and a cornea develops later, so adults have red pupils and red irises. In a non-white rabbit the gene for red eyes makes the coat dilute or paler than it is normally.

Another advantage of the wire pen is that food cannot come into contact with the hutch floor and thereby become soiled. Cleanliness is of great importance. A high standard of hygiene should be maintained at all times.

The food is placed in an automatic feeder or creep feeder. These feeders provide the rabbits with food 24 hours a day. The stockman has only to ensure that the hoppers are full at all times. Water should also be supplied in larger-than-normal quantities. An automatic watering system is used, ensuring a supply of fresh water at all times.

BREEDING RECORDS

The use of a breeding register is very important to the raiser of commercial rabbits. Attempting to keep the dates of matings and litters in the head of the stockman is an absolute waste of time. It is all too easy to forget these vital statistics. A regular record of all the matings, etc., should be written down and stored in some efficient recording system.

Most breeders use hutch cards that are pinned to the outside of the hutch. The information is then transferred into the recording system. However, the data recorded on the hutch card is still readily available to the stockman whenever he wishes to refer to it. It saves time because he is not forced to refer back to the recording system every time he wants a single date or the sire of a particular rabbit. The hutch card can be just a plain card or can be purchased specially printed for that purpose.

On the hutch card the stockman should enter the name of the doe, the name of its sire and dam and the date it was born. He should also record the date and sire of any litters born to the doe, the number in the litter, the number of live births, and the date they were born.

By keeping these records, the stockman will be able to tell which does produce the best litters, which does are suited to which bucks and from which mating a particular rabbit was produced. Also, he will be able to determine whether he is making any improvement in his herd and in which qualities his stock lacks or excels.

KILLING

If the commercial rabbit breeder wishes to sell his rabbits in the form of dressed meat, he will have to learn how to butcher his

stock in the correct manner, with the least amount of fuss and under hygienic conditions.

There are two basic ways of killing rabbits. The first is to kill the animal with a heavy instrument. The rabbit is placed on a table facing the stockman's left or right side. The rabbit's ears are held away from the neck with one hand, and the rabbit is hit with the instrument just behind the head at the nape of the neck. The stockman must take care that the blow does not come into contact with the rabbit's shoulders, or severe bruising of the flesh will result, making the carcass very unattractive.

Although death is instantaneous, the body may kick out for a few seconds after death. This is the reflex action of the rabbit's nerves. These kicks can be quite strong, as the hind legs will thresh through the full course of their total potential movement. Therefore, the rabbit should be held until it lies still. Very often with this method of slaughter the nose and ears may bleed, as the veins are ruptured.

The second method of slaughter, while equally efficient, requires more experience. The rabbit is grasped by the hind feet, with its head held downward. The other hand is placed under the chin, and the head is pulled out and down in one swift movement. The neck is dislocated, and death is instant. This action should be accomplished quickly but firmly; any undue pressure may pull the rabbit's head from the shoulders. This should never happen if the job is done properly.

It is important to remember that any stock to be killed should not be fed for 24 hours before the slaughter. This will ensure that there is no partly digested food in the rabbit's stomach when it is dressed.

DRESSING THE MEAT

Soon after killing, the rabbit should be pelted. If this task is left until the body becomes stiff, it is much harder to accomplish.

The body of the rabbit is hung from a nail on the wall by splitting the hocks and pushing the nail through them. If the pelt is to be used, it is essential that the pelting be done properly and cleanly. Many good pelts are ruined by lack of experience in this area.

It is a good idea to pin a plastic bag on the wall so that the rabbit hangs into it. The skin is then cut from each hock to the vent, tak-

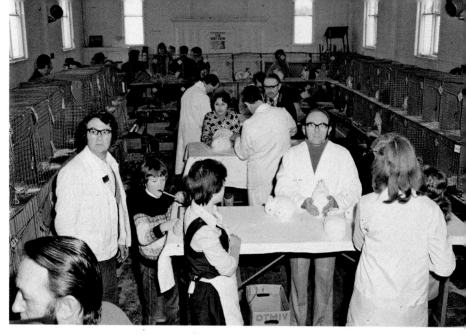

An over-all view of an English rabbit show.

A commercial breeder's rabbitry. Each cage is equipped with record pads. Without records it will be impossible to trace the ancestry and progeny of a litter.

ing care not to cut through into the flesh. The skin is taken from the legs by cutting around the thighs. While this is being done, the skin is pulled away slightly from the rump. It can then be pulled away from the rump towards the shoulders in one movement, after cutting off the tail.

The front legs are treated in a similar manner, and the skin from these parts is dropped into the plastic bag. If the head is to be taken off, the fur should be cut away from around the neck and the whole pelt taken from the rabbit. The newly taken pelt should be hung somewhere until it can receive proper attention. It should not be tossed aside or it will begin to deteriorate and be rendered useless.

The blood is now released from the carcass by cutting the veins in the neck. After this has been done, the color of the flesh will be much more pale. The stomach is opened from a point just in front of the vent up to the start of the rib cage. All the entrails are removed. The offal should fall into the plastic bag along with the rest of the waste. During disemboweling it is wise to ensure that the intestines are kept intact. If they are cut or ruptured, the bile will be released, which makes the job messy and somewhat smelly. The kidneys, heart and liver should be left inside the carcass. The gall bladder should be cut away from the liver, which is left intact for the same reason the intestines are not ruptured.

The forelimbs are cut off at the feet and the ends inserted into slits cut into the ribcage. There is no practical reason for this except that it makes the dressed carcass appear much neater. The hind limbs are severed at the hocks. One is inserted into the other through the tendon; this leg is, in turn, pushed through the tendon of the other leg. In this way the legs are held firmly and the thighs are pushed outward.

The finished carcass is then cleaned up without actually washing it. All the bloodstains are wiped off in addition to any other undesirable marks. A dressed carcass looks bad if it is uncleaned. Likewise, bruise marks on the flesh should be avoided.

In England, the dressed carcasses are packed into lined crates. The weights are recorded on a card that is stapled to the crate. In the United States, the carcasses are sometimes cut into pieces and sold as fryers. They are packaged in a carton marked with the weight of the product and the grade of meat.

The dressing-out loss is the difference between the live weight and the dead weight of the rabbit. The older a rabbit when it is slaughtered, the more the dressing-out loss. In the adult rabbit, this may be as high as 60 percent; in the younger rabbit it may be 50 percent or even lower. The more fat a meat rabbit carries, the higher the dressing-out loss.

MARKETING RABBIT MEAT

In England, rabbit meat is dressed and packaged by the farmer and sold directly to the butcher. In some cases the meat is sold to restaurants for use in delicacy dishes.

In the United States, the live rabbits are sometimes sold to a processing butcher. This is often a large concern that will kill, dress and pack the animals and then sell them to the customer. In these places the rabbits are put on a conveyer belt after they are killed and each job is done at certain points along the line.

For the rabbit raiser with only a small amount of stock, it would be advantageous to find a local market with a constant demand like a local butcher or hotel. The overhead could then be kept to a minimum and a small profit could be made.

It is of course possible to increase the price received for each dressed rabbit by selling directly to the ultimate user (eater, in this case) of the rabbit, but the extra time and effort required to do this probably are not worthwhile investing. In any event, selling rabbits as meat is a competitive, demanding enterprise, one subject to much regulation from health and food inspectors.

PELTS

The fur of the rex and often the satin rabbit is used by furriers. These pelts are often used in their natural state just as they are taken from the animal. The fur of other fur breeds, on the other hand, is processed. This means that it is pulled or the guard hairs are removed and then it is dried.

Various factors influence the way the fur is graded. For example, if the rabbit is in molt at the time of slaughter, the pelt will be affected. Likewise, if the pelt is from a young rabbit, the density will not be the same as from an adult rabbit.

Care should be taken when the pelt is removed from the carcass. A good pelt, especially from a white rabbit, can be easily spoiled or

A prize-winning sable/seal rex pelt on display along with its award and a novelty item. Demand for rabbit fur increases temporarily when a fur-trimmed novelty becomes popular.

stained by careless handling at this stage. After its removal, the pelt can either be left whole and placed on a stretcher or cut up the middle and nailed onto a board to dry.

Pelt stretchers are simple pieces of steel spring wire bent into a "U" shape. The pelt is placed over the forks of the "U" like a sleeve. The ends of the forks are then pulled together and held with a wire fastener.

The pelt that is to be nailed instead of stretched is placed fur side down on a flat board and the tail is removed. A one-inch nail is tacked into the root of the tail and the pelt is pulled slightly in the opposite direction, towards the neck, where another nail is

tacked. Nailing the pelt on each side will prevent creases. If the pelt is pulled too tightly, it will lose much of its density and be lowered in grade.

The next step is to remove all the fat and any flesh that may have been left behind when the pelt was removed. This is done with a blunt knife or stick by scraping the fat off, not pulling it. Once it is clean, the pelt should be removed from the board and hung somewhere airy to dry out naturally. Artificial heat should never be used, because the fur may be damaged. Drying can take as long as a week, but the normal time is about three to four days. The drying pelt should never be rolled up and stored, as that would cause the leather side to crack.

Dressing the pelt is really a job for the expert, but it can be done by the ordinary rabbit raiser if necessry. There are two main methods for curing the prepared rabbit pelt—the salt-acid process and the salt-alum process.

Salt-Acid Process: The salt-acid process requires one pound of common cooking salt dissolved in one gallon of water. While the salt and water solution is being stirred, one-half ounce of sulfuric acid is added. Metal containers should never be used for mixing the liquid, because the sulfuric acid will damage metal surfaces.

Great care should be taken to ensure that no acid comes into contact with the skin, especially the face or eyes. If any acid accidentally splashes onto the skin, wash with plenty of cold water and seek medical advice.

Once the acid has finished bubbling, it will have cooled and the solution will be ready for use. The entire pelt should be completely submerged in the solution for at least two days. During this time the pelt should be stirred occasionally to ensure that all parts of it come into contact with the liquid.

After two days the pelt should be removed and rinsed with plenty of cold water from a hose. The pelt is then washed in a solution of borax and water. One ounce of borax to a gallon of water should be sufficient. The pelt is then rinsed again and *squeezed* out. It should *not* be wrung, as this will damage the fur.

The damp pelt should then be put back onto the board and tacked down as if it were being stretched. This time, however, the pelt is nailed at one-inch intervals all the way around. When the

pelt has nearly dried but is still slightly damp, it should be rubbed with grease or oil. Butter can be used if grease or oil is unavailable. Before the pelt is completely dry, it should be manipulated by hand. This is achieved by removing the nails and pulling and stretching the skin over the edges of the board so that it becomes softened. This process must be repeated until the required softness is attained. If the pelt is still not soft enough after it is removed from the board, it should be wet with clean cold water, tacked down to the board again and the entire softening process repeated.

If the softened pelt is too greasy, it can be quickly immersed into a container of gasoline. The final stage is working the fur in a box of white sawdust. This will make the fur shine and add to its beauty.

Salt-Alum Process: The second method for curing the pelt is the salt-alum process. One pound of ammonia alum or potash alum is dissolved in one gallon of water. In another container, four ounces of washing soda and eight ounces of salt are dissolved into one half-gallon of water. The soda/salt solution is poured into the alum solution and stirred well. The entire solution is then mixed with enough flour to make a thin paste. (To avoid lumps, it is better to mix the flour with a little water before adding it to the solution.) The pelt is tacked out on the board as described.

This process is repeated two or three times with intervals of one day in between. Each day the previous day's paste is removed and a fresh layer is applied. The final coat of paste can be left on the pelt for two or three days. When this process has been completed, the pelt is removed and rinsed in the solution of borax and water described for the salt-acid process.

Skins cured by the salt-alum process are inclined to be much harder than with the first process. Therefore, the pelt will require much more work in order to make it soft and supple. But the rabbit furs prepared in this manner can be made into some very attractive novelty items by the fancier. Gloves, muffs, hats, etc., can be made and sold to friends and relatives. This will give the backyard rabbit fancier another source of income to offset the cost of keeping and feeding his stock.

ANGORA WOOL

The management of Angora rabbits for wool production is slightly different from that of other breeds of domestic rabbit. The breeder must take great care to ensure that the wool from the rabbit's coat does not come into contact with dirt and become soiled.

The method of feeding and the amount of the ration are basically the same, except that hay should not be provided in racks inside the hutch. Hay usually contains a certain amount of dust and seed that may get into the Angora's coat and be difficult to remove. Therefore the rack should be placed on the outside of the hutch door where the dust can fall onto the rabbitry floor.

Often the young bucks that are intended for wool production are castrated just after weaning. These rabbits are called "woollers" and can be kept together in one hutch to save space and time. They are sometimes kept with a number of does that also are woollers.

In one year, a good producer can get eight to ten inches—approximately one pound—of wool per rabbit. Angora rabbits that are well managed require very little grooming. The rabbits should be sheared every ten to twelve weeks. If the rabbit is left longer than this, the wool has a tendency to tangle and clog.

There are some basic pieces of equipment that the potential Angora breeder should obtain. A table of about waist height is necessary. The table legs should have casters so that the table can be turned in any direction without moving the rabbit. The table top should be about two feet square and should be covered with sacking or a piece of carpet, pile side down, so the rabbit can grip the top.

The grooming brush is of great importance. It should be of the finest quality, with single steel bristles set into a rubber pad. A good sharp pair of hairdressing scissors is also essential. When a large number of rabbits are to be sheared, a pair of electric shears is a must. Although the initial investment may be high, the shears will save much time and effort in the long run. Some type of ruler will be required to measure the length of wool taken from the rabbits. The breeder will also need suitable containers, one for each grade of wool. These containers must be airtight and clean. Each should have a label fixed to the lid to describe the grade of wool contained within.

Tools for grooming and cutting Angora rabbit wool.

During the grooming process, the rabbit is placed on the table and the wool is parted down the middle of the back. Each side is brushed with downward strokes to the ends. Then the ends of the wool are brushed up and out to remove any knots or foreign matter.

Each side is groomed in the same manner, moving the part farther down the side until the coat has had a really good brushing. The rabbit should then be removed from the table and held in the lap of the groomer so that the head, neck, belly and chest can be done in the same manner. Any wool that is hopelessly tangled or stained can be cut off as long as it is not a major part of the rabbit's coat.

An Angora rabbit with its wool being plucked.

Removing the Wool

There are three major methods for removing the wool from Angora rabbits. None of the methods offers any particular advantage; it is strictly a matter of personal preference. Young rabbits are usually sheared when they reach weaning age to get rid of the baby coat. The method used will depend on the number of rabbits to be sheared.

The first is the plucking method, whereby the wool is removed in three stages by pulling it from the rabbit. This method yields the highest grade of wool. The stockman must be very careful when plucking to ensure that only the loose hairs are pulled. One hand plucks the wool while the other is held against the skin.

The other two methods—shearing and clipping—are basically the same except for the tool that is used. Shearing is done with an electric clippers; clipping is done with a scissors.

The rabbit can either be held in the arms of the groomer to restrain it or it can be tied. The back is clipped first, one side at a time, then the belly, chest and neck. The groomer must exercise great care to make sure that the rabbit is not injured by the clippers or scissors.

The breeder can gain experience by practicing on an old breeding doe before shearing the woollers. After shearing, the rabbit should be thoroughly brushed to ensure that the new coat will grow straight and tangle-free.

The rabbit that has just been sheared will feel the extremes of cold temperature, so it should be given some kind of protection. This can be done by providing the rabbit with a nesting box lined with a suitable bedding such as flock from an old mattress. As the new coat grows, the bedding should be removed or it will become entangled within the new coat of wool.

The wool can also be cut or sheared.

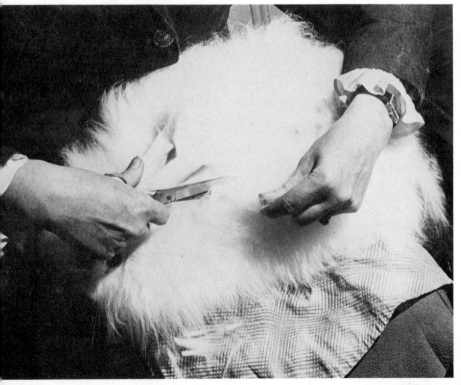

An Angora rabbit surrounded by an array of articles manufactured from Angora wool. The demand for this material is small in comparison to the demand for rabbit meat and other rabbit products and by-products, and Angoras are raised more for their beauty than commercial uses—but the skill of the artisian who can fashion such garments is admired.

A newly-sheared Angora rabbit is susceptible to colds, so the necessary precautions should be taken.

Grading Wool

Grade No. 1 wool is pure white, perfectly clean, free from all matting and two to three inches in length. Grade No. 2 wool is pure white, perfectly clean, free of all matting, and one and one-half to two inches in length. Grade No. 3 is pure white, perfectly clean, free from all matting, and one to one and one-half inches. Grade No. 4 is pure white, perfectly clean, matted wool of any length. Grade No. 5 is any soiled wool whether it is matted or not.

Wool should be stored in the airtight containers mentioned earlier. The containers should be placed in a bag with mothballs.

Ailments and Diseases

Throughout this book, particularly in the chapter on management, the emphasis has been on hygiene, for a very good reason. If the rabbitry is not kept clean at all times, it will become the target for dangerous germs and organisms that will quickly multiply.

Perfect hygiene is nearly impossible. For example, although the use of a separate sweeping brush for each hutch would be ideal and would restrict the spread of disease from one hutch to another, it would be impractical. Not many rabbitries are in a position to be able to use a different brush for each hutch. Total disinfection is also nearly impossible to achieve during the everyday cleaning out of the hutches.

However, there are many things that can be done to help restrict or minimize the spread of disease. The main one is to wash all tools and equipment whenever possible. These items should be washed every week without fail.

There are many types of disinfectants on the market from which the rabbit fancier can choose. The final choice will depend on the price and the use of the disinfectant which, in its undiluted form, must never come into contact with the rabbits. Many preparations contain properties that could poison a rabbit. If the disinfectant comes into contact with the rabbit's fur, the rabbit will try to clean it off and perhaps poison itself.

Whenever a new rabbit is introduced to the rabbitry, it should be kept in a quarantine hutch at a distance from the main hutches. The rabbit should be carefully watched for any signs of disease or illness. Should any be detected, the correct diagnosis should be made and the rabbit treated accordingly. The water and feeding pots used by this rabbit should never be mixed with those of the other rabbits.

DETECTING DISEASE

The experienced rabbit breeder will be able to detect any signs of disease in his stock from the outset. He will know his rabbits very well and will be able to tell whether one of them is not acting normal. Some signs are obvious. The state of the rabbit's droppings is the prime indication. If they are loose, the rabbit may have eaten something that has upset its stomach. If the droppings smell strong, there is something more serious than a stomach upset. The rabbit should be isolated for further observations. A healthy rabbit should have a clean nose and sparkling eyes; its coat should lie flat and smooth. If the rabbit sits hunched up with eyes closed, something is wrong. Steps should be taken to diagnose the complaint.

All of these measures are vital in the process of preventing the spread of disease. Prevention is always better than cure. Because correct diagnosis may be difficult for the novice, the advice of a more experienced breeder should be sought.

WRY NECK

Wry neck appears suddenly as the direct result of an injury to the inner ear and its sensitive organs. The rabbit can be of any age or sex. The head of the afflicted rabbit will fall to one side; in severe cases, the unfortunate animal will be unable to maintain its balance. The rabbit will walk in a circle, as it is unable to keep itself moving in a straight line.

The injury is almost certainly caused by the rabbit's rushing around its hutch in a state of excitement or panic. There is also evidence that wry neck can be caused by nervousness. Mild cases sometimes correct themselves within a few days, provided the patient is kept in a warm dry hutch and fed well. Bad cases are beyond recovery, and the rabbit should be destroyed.

ABSCESSES

The appearance of any kind of lump should be treated with suspicion. If an abscess is suspected, it should be left alone until it begins to weep. When this stage is reached, the rabbit's fur should be carefully removed from the region around the site of the abscess.

The lump should be swabbed with a lint pad soaked in antiseptic, and an incision should be made at the lower part of the abscess. The cut will allow the pus in the abscess to drain fully during treatment. The patient should be restrained with the help of another person and the pus gently squeezed out of the sore until all traces of it have been removed.

The pus that is extracted should be burnt well away from the rabbitry, as it can become the source of reinfection if it is allowed to come into contact with an open cut or scratch.

The wound should then be washed out with a lint pad soaked in the antiseptic and dressed with tincture of iodine. The wound should be inspected every other day and a fresh dressing applied. Once the wound has healed, the fur should grow normally again.

Milkweed Poisoning

Some dried hay in the United States may contain milkweed. It grows only in American meadows and prairies. Dried or fresh, it is toxic to all rabbits.

After eating the hay containing the weed, the rabbit will become paralyzed. The back may arch and the head drop between the front legs. This affliction has been termed "head down disease." The amount of paralysis depends on the amount of milkweed eaten. In severe cases, the whole body becomes completely paralyzed. In mild cases, only the head and neck muscles are affected.

Treatment is very slow and painful for the rabbit. The patient should be induced to eat and drink as often as possible to gain enough strength to fight off the poison.

COLDS

The common cold can become a great nuisance if it is not treated promptly. As with humans, there is no miracle cure. All that can be done is to make the patient as comfortable as possible.

Rabbits that are suffering from colds will sneeze and shake their heads in an attempt to clear the nasal passages. There will also be a discharge from the nose, and the rabbit will wipe its face with its forepaws to try and clean this mucus away. The fur on the inside of the front legs will become soaked with mucus, after which it will mat and become quite hard.

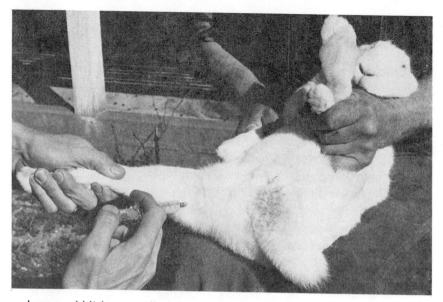

Large rabbitries usually have a veterinarian on their staff. Givng routine inoculations is just one of his many tasks to keep the stock in condition and free from devastating diseases.

Sneezing may also result from irritation from dust or hay. Once a cold has been discharged, the rabbit should be housed well away from the main rabbitry. It is preferable to house the patient in a hutch that is warm and dry and also has a free flow of fresh air without any drafts.

The amount of pelleted food should be reduced and fresh green-food fed in its place. The use of nasal drops is futile, because the rabbit will sneeze them out before they can take effect. A mixture of eucalyptus oil and camphor oil should be applied to the inside of the nostrils with a small paintbrush. This will help the rabbit to breathe and also ensure that the mucus is kept flowing from the nasal passages instead of drying and blocking the nose. The oil mixture can also be applied to all hutch surfaces, such as the litter board, that are likely to come into contact with the rabbit.

If the rabbit is a valuable asset to the rabbitry, the breeder should persevere until the cold clears. It may take some time, but the rabbit will be useful again. A rabbit suffering from a cold should never come into contact with unaffected stock and should never, therefore, be mated.

EYE INFECTIONS

The domestic rabbit is quite susceptible to infections of the eye. The most common complaint is inflammation of the tear duct. This can be caused by dust or other foreign matter trapped in the region of the tear duct and blocking it completely. The eye pocket fills up with water that overflows and runs down the rabbit's cheek.

Usually only one eye is affected; both eyes, however, may become infected. The fur in the region of the eye and cheek will become wet and matted. Sometimes the fur in the eye area falls off, exposing skin that becomes chapped and sore. Treatment consists of regular eye baths using an aqueous solution of boric acid. The weak solution should be applied with a piece of lint or cotton wool. Human eye ointments have also been used successfully.

Other eye complaints can be caused by drafts, injury during fighting and accidents. Sometimes baby rabbits are slow in opening their eyes after the usual 10-day stage. If the eye appears to be inflamed and sore, it should be bathed in a very weak solution of boric acid and warm water. During bathing, the eyelids will become quite soft and usually can be easily pried apart with gentle pressure from the fingers.

PNEUMONIA

Although pneumonia is rare in the rabbit, it does sometimes appear after the onset of another disease or illness. The rabbit may be so weakened by the onslaught of an illness that it has no resources to fight off pneumonia. A sudden change in temperature can also reduce the rabbit's resistance. Good feeding and management are usually enough to keep pneumonia at bay, even during illness.

The affected animal will hold its head back in an attempt to breathe. Mucus may appear around the mouth and nose. The rabbit's appetite will decrease, and it will become listless and uninterested in anything that is going on around it.

It is far safer to cull the rabbit as soon as the symptoms are diagnosed. But if the rabbit is valuable, it should be treated with injections that can be obtained from the local veterinary surgeon. Homemade treatments are not satisfactory, and time is of the greatest importance in these cases. Untreated rabbits will die after a few days.

SORE HOCKS

A sore hock is a simple matter in itself, but if it is not treated in its early stages it will become very serious indeed. Sore hock is caused when the fur is rubbed away from under the hind feet of the rabbit. The skin becomes sore and cracked, sometimes breaking out into scabs which become infected with foreign matter.

Rex rabbits are perhaps more susceptible to sore hocks than any other breed. If the rabbits are not supplied with adequate bedding, the animals will wear away the surface of the foot pad from the toe end to the ankle joint. The rex rabbit has only a thin covering of fur in this area.

The larger breeds of rabbit are more susceptible than the smaller breeds, because they have much more slender foot pads and much more bulk to carry. The smaller breeds have a relatively larger foot pad area. Active rabbits of any size can develop sore hocks, especially young and mature bucks that are constantly stamping their feet. The foot becomes bruised and sore and the infection sets in very quickly if it is not treated.

The rabbit that is suffering from sore hocks will be loath to move around the hutch. Vitality is reduced.

The affected area of the foot should be kept clean at all times; antiseptic ointment should be applied liberally. A good, deep bed of straw should be supplied to reduce further injury to the foot pads.

SLOBBERS

Slobbers is a secondary infection caused by abscesses in the rabbit's mouth. The abscess can be caused by a broken or bad tooth or by a simple infection of the gums.

The affected rabbit will drool at the mouth, causing the saliva to run down the lower jaw and onto the chest, where the fur will become matted. The general appetite will decrease, and the animal will quickly go out of condition. Little can be done for infections of the mouth and the rabbit should be culled.

VENT DISEASE

Vent disease is sometimes referred to as hutch burn. It is reportedly caused by dirt that makes contact with the vent tissue

around the sex organ. The skin in this area becomes very sore. Scabs appear and then burst, spreading pus all over the area.

Rabbits that suffer from it are reluctant to mate. If they do mate, the infection can be passed from buck to doe or vice versa. The disease is not hereditary, nor can it be passed from rabbit to man or to any other animal.

Treatment consists of washing the affected area with a mild solution of soapy water and drying thoroughly. Lanolin ointment is then applied to the skin and rubbed in. Recovery is slow, but it can be achieved.

SCABBY FACE

Scabby face is another secondary infection. It is reportedly caused by the rabbit's taking pellets from the anus during coprophagy while it is suffering from vent disease. The skin around the nose and face becomes infected with bacteria and breaks into sores and scabs.

Treatment consists of giving the afflicted rabbit an injection of 150,000 units of penicillin G procaine in oil. The rabbit can become reinfected even after this treatment, and it will not clear until the vent disease has been eradicated.

WORMS

Some of the worms that infect rabbits are the same worms that are carried by cats and dogs. The eggs are picked up by the rabbit in contaminated food or bedding. Once an egg enters the body, it attaches itself to the internal organs, where it hatches out. The young worms feed upon the food that the rabbit eats, causing the body to lose condition quickly. Sometimes the adult worm is passed through the anus.

All dogs and cats should be kept well away from the rabbitry and should never be allowed to come into contact with the foodstuffs or bedding that are intended for use in the rabbitry. Dogs and cats should never be allowed to lie on bales of hay. A rabbit with worms should be isolated and the rabbitry disinfected.

MUCOID ENTERITIS

Mucoid enteritis is also referred to as bloat or scours. The affected rabbit loses condition within a matter of hours after becom-

ing infected. The rabbit's fur becomes rough and tangled; the eyes squint and are dull and swollen. Diarrhea or constipation may or may not be present.

The rabbit wastes away and may weigh only a fraction of its normal weight. Young rabbits that are diseased in this way sit next to the water pot in a hunched position. In extreme cases, they will sit with their front paws dangling in the water. In this position they will take frequent small sips of water from the pot. The stomach becomes distended and bloated, giving the disease its name. The end result is usually death. Rabbits that do recover are not immune to the disease and can become reinfected. There is no simple treatment. Some pellets contain an antibiotic that helps to reduce the incidence of this disease.

MALOCCLUSION

Malocclusion or buck teeth is a result of misalignment of the top and bottom sets of front teeth. Normally these teeth should meet and wear away at the extreme edges; therefore it is important that they wear away naturally.

If the edges of the teeth do not meet, the teeth will continue to grow until they appear like elephant's tusks. The teeth will grow out of the mouth and can reach tremendous proportions if left unchecked. Constant trimming will help keep the teeth in good condition in mild cases. In severe cases, the rabbit should be culled as it will be unable to feed itself.

Malocclusion is hereditary. Any rabbits passing on this trait should be removed from the breeding pen.

The Netherland dwarf is more susceptible to buck teeth because of the flat nature of its face.

MASTITIS

Mastitis more often affects suckling does than does that are not rearing young. The disease is caused by an infection of the mammary glands by staphylococcal bacteria.

The teats of the suckling doe become inflamed and very sore. At a later stage they may turn blue. The mammary glands swell considerably and appear very hard and lumpy. An injection of penicillin by a veterinary surgeon is the normal treatment. The infection is more easily cured if caught in its early stages. If it is left

until the more advanced stages, complete cure is almost impossible. The rabbit should be culled.

All nest boxes, hutches and equipment used by the doe must be thoroughly sterilized and the corpse of the rabbit burned.

FLEAS AND TICKS

Fleas and ticks should never appear on a domestic rabbit. Good management will ensure that the rabbits are kept healthy and clean. It is possible that a visiting rabbit could bring these pests and deposit them among its hosts. Although rabbits that are tended properly should never carry these parasites, one can never be too careful.

Constant scratching should be viewed with great suspicion. Prompt action must be taken should it be discovered that a rabbit has fleas or ticks. A dusting powder specially formulated for small animals can be bought from any good pet store. Preparations intended for dogs should never be used as they can be too severe, causing irritation of the rabbit's skin.

Flea powder should be used for three days in succession to ensure that all the insects and their eggs are completely destroyed.

MYXOMATOSIS

Myxomatosis is certainly the most well-known rabbit disease. It is horrible in its affliction and deadly in its action. There is some controversy over the actual carrier of this viral disease. Some have laid the blame on the common rabbit flea, while others maintain that it is carried by the mosquito or other flying insects.

Immunization is possible if there is an outbreak in the locality of the rabbitry. This can be an expensive proposition and is not always guaranteed to keep the disease at bay. Precautions should always be taken against the entry of flying insects into the rabbitry. Fine mesh netting can be used to cover all the doors and windows. Fly sprays should not be used, as they can prove toxic to small animals. Fly repellents giving off a vapor to kill insects should only be used in a large area where there is an abundant supply of fresh air. Old-fashioned fly paper is still the best method of controlling the number of insects within the rabbitry. These strips of paper are coated with a sticky substance.

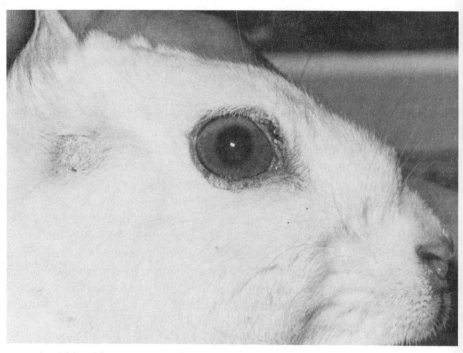

A rabbit with symptoms of myxomatosis, a viral disease transmitted by mosquitos. Notice the abscess at the base of the ear and the swelling in front of the eye.

Any rabbit suspected of suffering from myxomatosis should be separated from its fellows. A veterinarian should be contacted. The infected rabbit will develop sores and scabs around the anus, the ears, eyes, nose and mouth. Just before death, the rabbit's veins will harden and the lungs will become congested. The afflicted rabbit will be unable to keep its balance while moving and will quickly die.

EXTERNAL INJURIES

Accidents occasionally happen within the rabbitry, resulting in the injury of a rabbit. Most accidents are the result of dropping a rabbit while it is being carried or allowing it to wander off the edge of a table or bench. Usually the rabbit receives nothing more serious than a shock. However, if the rabbit falls awkwardly, it could fracture a limb. If a fracture is suspected, the rabbit should be placed somewhere dry and warm to minimize the effect of

shock. A thorough inspection of all the rabbit's limbs will establish the extent of the injury and its exact location. Such an injury should not be treated at home. The fancier should seek the services of a qualified veterinarian. In addition to setting the limb properly, a vet will be able to detect any internal injuries that may not be apparent to the layman.

Cuts and lacerations can be treated on the spot by the handler. The wound should be cleaned with a lint pad soaked in antiseptic. Any fur in the locality of the wound should be carefully cut away with a sharp pair of scissors. If the wound is deep and bleeds despite all efforts to stem the flow of blood, it would be wise to contact a veterinary surgeon who will stitch the wound.

Covering a wound with a bandage is futile, because the rabbit will merely chew it away. If the wound is kept clean and free from dust and dirt, it will heal satisfactorily within a few days.

CANNIBALISM

Suckling does will eat their young for no apparent reason, even when the youngsters are up to ten days of age. It is very upsetting to the new fancier, but the more experienced rabbit breeder will take such things in stride. Normally, when the doe is well fed, there is little trouble. However, some does will kill and eat their young no matter how well fed. If the doe is persistent in eating all her young she should be disposed of, because this trait can be passed on from generation to generation. Fostering should be considered only if the doe is particularly valuable in the breeding pen.

Maiden does will sometimes eat their newborn young in a frenzied attempt to clean up the nest. Such inexperienced rabbits can be forgiven for this mistake, because they will usually rear subsequent litters without any further trouble.

Excessive handling of newborn baby rabbits will sometimes make the doe nervous, and she will kill all her young without actually eating them. This is understandable; the blame rests with the stockman for his bad management and lack of common sense.

Organizations

THE AMERICAN RABBIT BREEDERS ASSOCIATION

The American Rabbit Breeders Association or the A.R.B.A., as it is commonly called, was created as the governing body of a handful of rabbit breeders in Illinois about 1915. The initial idea behind the A.R.B.A. was to organize a group that would safeguard the interests of the ordinary rabbit breeder who kept and reared rabbits chiefly as a hobby.

Standards were drawn up by the founding members of the association to maintain a high level of quality within the types of rabbit bred by the members. The standards were intended to provide all fanciers with an ideal and also to ensure that all nominated judges used the same standards.

Today the A.R.B.A. has a membership of over 10,000 fanciers from all walks of life who live throughout the United States. The association caters to all aspects of rabbit-raising, including exhibition rabbits, commercial rabbits, pelt-producing rabbits and, of course, the ever-popular pet rabbit.

Incorporated within the A.R.B.A. are the breed specialist clubs that cater exclusively to one breed. These clubs hold stock shows within the pen shows organized by regional clubs and offer special prizes for the best specimens of that particular breed.

The American youth program is an important aspect of the A.R.B.A. It is, in fact, a junior A.R.B.A. run along lines similar to those of parent organization. All young fanciers should consider taking part in the activities of the youth section.

Many hundreds of local or regional clubs are affiliated with the A.R.B.A. Each has its own A.R.B.A. representative. The states are also grouped together into districts for which there are provincial A.R.B.A. representatives.

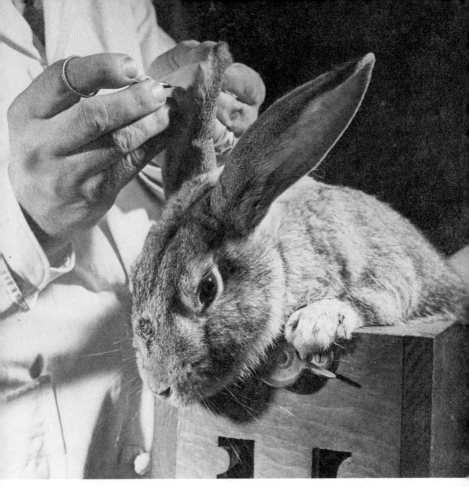

A breeder can identify his stock by a simple pen type tattooing needle seen here or by a plier type tattooing device.

A herd book in which all the particulars of every rabbit registered with the organization are listed is kept at the head office of the A.R.B.A. Rabbits are categorized before they are registered. **Scrub** rabbits are those that cannot be identified as to their breed. **Grade** rabbits can be identified as to breed but do not have purebred parents. **Purebred** rabbits can be traced back along their pedigrees for at least three generations. Finally, the **registered** rabbits are the true aristocrats of the American rabbit world. These rabbits have pedigrees that stretch much further back. They are registered on the rolls of the A.R.B.A. and can be identified by a tattoo mark in the ear.

A registered rabbit carries a registration certificate providing details of the rabbit's tattoo number, its date of birth, the name of the breeder and the name of the owner, if different from that of the breeder. The certificate also carries a brief description of the rabbit and its color.

The final category of rabbits is **full pedigree.** All pedigree rabbits are registered with a district registrar appointed by the A.R.B.A. The registrar tattoos a number on the rabbit's ear and awards a seal. The seal is a form of grading. A red seal indicates that both the parents of the rabbit are registered. A red and white seal means that the first and second generations have been registered. A red, white and blue seal indicates that the full pedigree has been registered with the A.R.B.A. The seal is attached to the registration certificate and sent to the head office of the organization to be stored for reference.

Grand championship certificates are awarded to rabbits that comply with certain regulations regarding their wins at shows. The championship is awarded in a series of legs. The rabbit must complete at least three legs before it can be considered for the supreme award. The legs are as follows:

1. Wins first in a class of not less than five entries owned by not less than three exhibitors.
2. Wins best of breed or best of variety with five rabbits shown in the breed or variety by at least three exhibitors.
3. Wins best opposite sex or best opposite sex of variety, providing there are five or more of the same sex as the winner shown in the breed or variety by at least three exhibitors.
4. Wins best in show.
5. Two legs cannot be honored for the same show on the same animal.
6. At least one of the wins must be obtained as an intermediate or a senior, and the awards are to be placed under at least two different A.R.B.A. judges.
7. No award can be counted unless it is attained in a regularly sanctioned A.R.B.A. show, with an A.R.B.A.-licensed judge placing the award.
8. The leg for the grand champion must be obtained by the exhibtor from the show secretary where the award was won.

Only one grand championship can be conferred on any one particular rabbit.

The A.R.B.A. publishes a magazine devoted to the breeding and showing of rabbits. The magazine *Domestic Rabbits* includes articles on the various breeds and all aspects of breeding rabbits, plus full news coverage of all coming events concerned with the A.R.B.A. and its affiliated clubs. There are also advertisements offering rabbit breeding and showing stock for sale. Details of the A.R.B.A. can be obtained by writing to American Rabbit Breeders Association, 24011 East Oakland Avenue, Bloomington, Illinois 61701.

THE BRITISH RABBIT COUNCIL

The British Rabbit Council, or BRC as it is more often called, is the British equivalent of the A.R.B.A. The BRC was formed by the amalgamation of a number of smaller rabbit clubs in about 1934. The total membership of the BRC runs into many hundreds of thousands of fanciers from all over the United Kingdom and even boasts members from other parts of the world.

There are about one thousand local rabbit clubs affiliated with the BRC and about 100 specialist breed clubs that cater to one breed of rabbit each.

The whole of the British rabbit fancy is governed by the BRC under a set of rules drawn up by the general committee. The show rules and breed standards are laid down by the BRC for the guidance of all fanciers in running shows, judging rabbits and exhibiting rabbits.

The BRC encourages the showing of rabbits and awards each show a star according to the grading of the show. The grade will depend upon the classification or schedule of the breeds to be shown. A **one-star show** will display the basic standard of classes that does not have to include a class for every breed of rabbit. A **two-star show** provides the same type of schedule but offers better prize money guaranteed at a certain level. A **three-star show** caters to all breeds and also guarantees a basic level of prize money. A **five-star show** is a classic, with at least one class for every breed of rabbit covered by the standards of the BRC.

Each rabbit that wins its breed class will be eligible to compete for a challenge certificate (C.C.), an award presented to the rabbit

that in the judge's opinion is the best of each breed or different color of each breed. For example, in the Polish classes there is a C.C. for the best red-eyed white Polish and one for the best any other color (AOC) Polish. Generally speaking, the C.C. will be awarded to any adult. However, the adult may be inferior or the under-five-month class winner may be so outstanding that it will take the C.C. from the adult. The idea is to have a rabbit that excels in all points and is in perfect condition coatwise.

A rabbit must accumulate 15 stars to become a silver star winner. The stars are awarded according to the grading of the shows where the C.C.'s were won. The fifteen stars must include at least two wins at a two-star show.

A rabbit that goes further will have to win 25 stars before it can be considered a champion. These stars have to include at least two wins at three-star shows. A rabbit that wins a total of 35 stars or more is considered a gold star certificate winner and a supreme champion.

All open shows covered by the BRC have to be staged so that the rabbits are placed in pens prior to being brought out by the pen stewards and placed before the BRC-approved judge. Local clubs also run box shows, small shows solely for the interest of the rabbit fancier. Competition is not as heavy at these shows. They give fanciers a chance to meet other breeders and chat about all aspects of rabbit keeping. The rabbits entered in box shows are not placed in pens, as at pen shows, but are left in their traveling boxes—hence the term box show. Each box is numbered at the beginning of the show. Local show diplomas are awarded by the BRC at box shows for the best rabbit in the show.

The BRC has area advisers whose task it is to answer any questions about the BRC.

Metal rings or bands are issued by the BRC for the identification of rabbits at shows. The rings are made of a hard, light metal and are slipped over the rabbit's foot soon after it leaves the nest and is weaned. The ring is pushed up the leg of the rabbit until it passes over the hock joint or ankle. As the rabbit grows, the ankle joint will also grow, making it impossible for the ring to slip off.

Embossed on each ring are the initials BRC, the year that the ring was issued and a letter to signify the group of breeds for which the ring should be used. For example, the Netherland

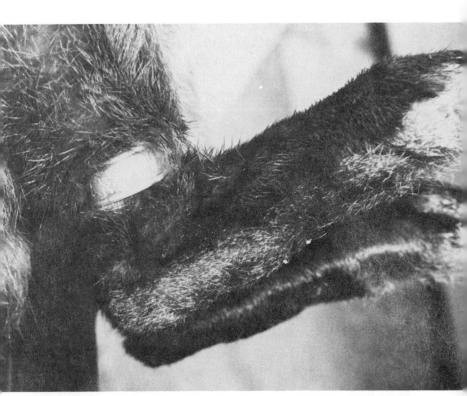

A British Rabbit Council registration ring on a rabbit's leg. The ring is permanent and cannot be reused. It is destroyed if the rabbit dies or has to be culled from the stock.

dwarf wears a ring with the letter X. A Dutch wears a ring with the letter B, and a Polish wears the letter A. Each ring also has a serial number, usually containing five digits. The serial number is recorded by the BRC when the ring is sold to the fancier. Once a ring has been used on one rabbit, it can never be used again on another rabbit if the first rabbit was entered in competition. If the rabbit must be culled, the ring must be destroyed along with the rabbit's body.

The official magazine of the BRC, *Fur and Feather,* is published fortnightly and contains all the latest show reports and also articles of interest to rabbit fanciers.

Details of the BRC activities can be obtained by writing to the British Rabbit Council, Purfoy House, 7 Kirkgate, Newark, Nottingham, England.

317

THE COMMERCIAL RABBIT ASSOCIATION

The Commercial Rabbit Association is a British club that caters exclusively to the interests of the commercial rabbit raiser in the United Kingdom. The association links all parties concerned with the industry to enhance the objectives of rabbit farmers. Food manufacturers play a large role, making it possible for the rabbit farmer to attend lectures given by notable persons connected with the various firms. Courses on improving his stock are also available to the farmer.

The Commercial Rabbit Association publishes a magazine, *Commercial Rabbit*, which covers all aspects of the industry both in the U.K. and abroad. Further details about the Commercial Rabbit Association can be obtained by writing to Cone Publications, Crondall Cottage, Highclere, Newbury, Berkshire, England.

I cannot recommend strongly enough that you join a national rabbit association. The amount of money it will cost you to join is very modest indeed when you consider the great benefits that are to be derived. You will be kept completely up to date with all of the happenings in the rabbit world, and in addition to all of the good advice you receive that can be put to use in raising better rabbits you'll also receive many money-saving tips that in a short while will more than recompense you for the membership fee. The people involved with the national societies and their publications are knowledgeable, dedicated, experienced rabbit fanciers. They know what they are talking about and are willing to help other fanciers overcome the obstacles that they have faced during their long experience. It would be silly for anyone interested in rabbits not to become an active member of the rabbit-raising fraternity by joining a society; for the sake of your animals and for your own enhanced enjoyment (and profit, if that's what you're looking for) from rabbit-raising, get into a national society. When writing to a society to obtain information and applications, you should enclose a self-addressed stamped envelope that can be used to mail your information to you; the societies are non-profit organizations and don't have big budgets allocated for enrolling new members.

Index

(Page references printed in bold indicate illustrations or photos. This is an index to topics only; breed references and illustrations are indexed on the following page.)

Rabbit Breeds